PLIN
ON HIM

SELECTIONS FROM THE LETTERS OF PLINY
ILLUSTRATING HIS LIFE AND CHARACTER

CHOSEN AND EDITED BY

H. A. B. WHITE, M.A.

Published by Bristol Classical Press (U.K.)
and by
Bolchazy-Carducci Publishers (U.S.A.)

Printed in Great Britain
First published in 1965 by
G. Bell & Son Ltd.
Reprinted in 1988 by:

U.K.	U.S.A.
Bristol Classical Press	Bolchazy-Carducci Publishers
226 North Street	44 Lake Street
Bedminster	Oak Park
Bristol BS3 1JD	IL 60302
ISBN 1-85399-036-1	ISBN 0-86516-212-3

NOTE

THIS selection follows the general plan adopted in some other volumes in the series. Pliny has written much to interest middle-school pupils, if they can be sufficiently helped over the difficulties. The notes are therefore designed to simplify the more obscure points of grammar and allusion.

The text is substantially that of the Loeb Classical Library volumes on Pliny, by kind permission of William Heinemann Ltd.

CONTENTS

INTRODUCTION

PLINY's star is now in the ascendant. Several years ago he was voted by a class of graduates the most popular but least read of all the Roman writers studied in English schools. Today it is doubtful whether he is still the least read.

What, then, is the reason for his popularity? Certainly, it is not that his writing is the easiest to translate. Again, he cannot rival Cicero's style and genuine fire of expression. He is unable to recount the military exploits of a Caesar and he does not possess the historical powers of a Livy. Perhaps the main charm of Pliny's letters is their variety of subject-matter in which both interest in and enjoyment of everyday life are fully expressed. He is no heroic figure. He has the same kind of virtues and faults as we have today. His topics are often as applicable to the twentieth century as to the first. In short, Pliny is one of us.

I. PLINY'S PRIVATE LIFE

Publius Caecilius Secundus was born at Novum Comum, on Lake Como in Northern Italy, in late A.D. 61 or early A.D. 62, during the reign of the notorious emperor Nero. His father died when he was very young and he was brought up under the guardianship of the famous Verginius Rufus who might easily have become emperor, had he so desired. He was adopted by his uncle, the Elder Pliny, and was given a first class education, during which he studied under the writer Quintilian, the Stoic philosophers, Euphrates and Artemidorus, and came to count as his personal friends many men of letters, including the famous historian, Tacitus, and Martial, the writer of epigrams.

Like his uncle, whose name he assumed when adopted by him, Pliny was of a bookish nature. He tells us that he wrote a Greek tragedy at the age of 14. Fortunately, however, he did not become as great a pedant as his uncle, although he led a life of study.

When his uncle died in the eruption of Vesuvius, A.D. 79, Pliny became his heir. Both his mother and his father had been comfortably situated, and now Pliny found himself immensely rich, the possessor of several country estates.

At this time, he started his career in law, which led to another in public life, to be described later. He also married several times and lived a very happy life with Calpurnia, his third wife, but was disappointed in his hope of children.

Although we should bear in mind that the only information we receive about his private life comes from Pliny himself in the letters which—unlike Cicero's—were thoroughly revised with an eye to publication, we can glean from this information that he was a loyal, generous, upright and conscientious citizen, a successful professional man and a very affectionate husband. True, he was also pedantic, prone to affectation, over-meticulous in style, and vain to the extent that he wished to win for himself a name in history, but surely his virtues outweighed his vices in an age which had none too high a moral code. Suffice it to say that Pliny affords us an example of the typical Roman gentleman who showed great humanity to those who worked under him.

II. PLINY'S PUBLIC LIFE

If we examine the main events in Pliny's Life (page 4), we may find it hard to accept the fact that Pliny is considered to have been a very ordinary kind of man.   Perhaps credit is not always given to his courage in conducting cases against informers in the Centumviral courts, as well as those dealing with questions of inheritance.   It is true that the consulship was not such a prize in imperial times as under the Republic, but Pliny also won the unique honour of being the first man to pass direct from a post as head of the Military Treasury to that of head of the Public Treasury.   Since he could satisfy emperors of such opposed temperaments as Domitian and Trajan, he must have possessed considerable ability.

III. Pliny's Times

Pliny lived in most stirring days, when human life was cheap and persecutions by tyrannical emperors commonplace.   He narrowly escaped death under Domitian, who conducted a purge of his Stoic friends. Pliny himself tells us that the informer Metius Carus actually brought charges against him, and that documents directed against Pliny were found in Domitian's desk after that emperor's assassination in A.D. 96. Certainly, Pliny must have faced serious risks in prosecuting informers and those accused of maladministration.

Under Nerva and Trajan, life became more settled, but it should still be noted that Pliny resisted the temptations of a lax age and was able to live an exemplary private life.

IV. Pliny's Style

Pliny consciously made Cicero his model and most nearly of the Silver Age writers mastered it.   The result is elegant but rather formal prose.   The style is polished, but self conscious, the figures of speech, such as antithesis, or contrast, and repetition are forcibly presented to us, and the great variety in vocabulary sometimes appears artificially contrived. Beginners in reading Pliny should be on their guard for the omission of the verb 'to be', for historic infinitives and for figures of speech, such as chiasmus, that are explained in the notes.

THE MAIN EVENTS IN PLINY'S LIFE

A.D.

61 or 62	Born at Novum Comum.
—	Adopted by his uncle at an early age, following the death of his father.
79	Witnessed the eruption of Vesuvius in which his uncle died. Assumed his uncle's name, 'Pliny'.
80	Started his legal career.
81	Served as military tribune in Syria.
89	Quaestor under Domitian.
91	Tribune.
93	Praetor. Prefect of the Military Treasury.
96	Prefect of the Public Treasury, under Nerva.
100	Consul *suffectus*, Sept.–Oct.
103	Augur.
105	President of commission to work on improving the banks and bed of the Tiber and to look after the drainage of the City. Member of Privy Council under Trajan.
111–113	Governor of Bithynia.
c. 113	Death.

PLINY ON HIMSELF

PLINY, THE LETTER WRITER

I

Pliny explains that he has been asked to publish a selection of his letters and has done so. He hopes that neither the friend who suggested publishing nor he himself will have cause to repent such a step and he hopes to increase the selection. It should be noted that, whilst Cicero wrote with no eye to the publication of his letters, Pliny writes rather self-consciously, realising that his words will be open to the scrutiny of future generations.

C. Plinius Secundus Septicio Suo S. — *salutem dat*

Frequenter hortatus es ut epistulas, si quas paulo accuratius scripsissem, colligerem publicaremque. Collegi, non servato temporis ordine (neque enim historiam componebam), sed ut quaeque in manus 5 venerat. Superest ut nec te consilii nec me paeniteat obsequii. Ita enim fiet ut eas, quae adhuc neglectae iacent, requiram, et, si quas addidero, non supprimam. Vale.

I, I

THE AFFECTIONATE HUSBAND

II

It would appear that Pliny was married three times, but we have little information about his first two marriages. It seems that he was very young when he married for the first time and that his second wife died about 97 A.D.

5

The next three letters describe his very happy third marriage. Calpurnia proved a very devoted wife. She probably survived him.

Incredibile est quanto desiderio tui tenear. In causa amor primum, deinde quod non consuevimus abesse. Inde est quod magnam partem noctium in imagine tua vigil exigo, inde, quod interdiu, quibus
5 horis te visere solebam, ad diaetam tuam ipsi me, ut verissime dicitur, pedes ducunt; quod denique aeger et maestus ac similis excluso, vacuo limine recedo. Unum tempus his tormentis caret, quo in foro et amicorum litibus conteror. Aestima tu, quae vita
10 mea sit, cui requies in labore, in miseria curisque solacium. Vale.

VII, 5

III

Scribis te absentia mea non mediocriter adfici unumque habere solacium quod pro me libellos meos teneas, saepe etiam in vestigio meo colloces. Gratum est quod nos requiris, quod his fomentis adquiescis.
5 Invicem ego epistulas tuas lectito atque identidem in manus quasi novas sumo; sed eo magis ad desiderium tui accendor. Nam, cuius litterae tantum habent suavitatis, huius sermonibus quantum dulcedinis inest! Tu tamen frequentissime scribe, licet
10 hoc ita me delectet, ut torqueat. Vale.

VI, 7

IV

Pliny sends a glowing account of his wife's virtues to Calpurnia's aunt and attributes in part to her the success of their married life.

Cum sis pietatis exemplum fratremque optimum et amantissimum tui pari caritate dilexeris, filiamque eius ut tuam diligas, nec tantum amitae ei verum etiam patris amissi adfectum repraesentes, non dubito maximo tibi gaudio fore, cum cognoveris dignam patre, 5 dignam te, dignam avo evadere. Summum est acumen, summa frugalitas. Amat me, quod castitatis indicium est. Accedit his studium litterarum quod ex mei caritate concepit. Meos libellos habet, lectitat, ediscit etiam. Qua illa sollicitudine cum videor 10 acturus, quanto, cum egi, gaudio adficitur! Disponit qui nuntient sibi adsensum, quos clamores excitarim, quem eventum iudicii tulerim. Eadem, si quando recito, in proximo discreta velo sedet, laudesque nostras avidissimis auribus excipit. Versus quidem 15 meos cantat etiam formatque cithara, non artifice aliquo docente, sed amore, qui magister est optimus.

His ex causis in spem certissimam adducor perpetuam nobis maioremque in dies futuram esse concordiam. 20 Non enim aetatem meam aut corpus, quae paulatim occidunt ac senescunt, sed gloriam diligit. Nec aliud decet tuis manibus educatam, tuis praeceptis institutam, quae nihil in contubernio tuo viderit nisi sanctum honestumque, quae denique amare me ex 25 tua praedicatione consueverit. Nam, cum matrem meam parentis loco verereris, me a pueritia statim formare, laudare, talemque, qualis nunc uxori meae videor, ominari solebas. Certatim ergo tibi gratias agimus, ego quod illam mihi, illa quod me sibi 30 dederis, quasi invicem elegeris. Vale.

IV, 19

PLINY'S WAY OF LIFE

V

*Pliny describes a typical summer-day routine of a Roman
author on his country estate; an early rise, meditation
behind closed shutters, then dictation to his secretary of what
he has composed.*

Quaeris quem ad modum in Tuscis diem aestate
disponam.

Evigilo cum libuit, plerumque circa horam primam,
saepe ante, tardius raro.   Clausae fenestrae manent.
5 Mire enim silentio et tenebris ab iis quae avocant,
abductus et liber et mihi relictus, non oculos animo
sed animum oculis sequor, qui eadem quae mens
vident, quotiens non vident alia.   Cogito, si quid in
manibus, cogito ad verbum scribenti emendantique
10 similis nunc pauciora, nunc plura, ut vel difficile,
vel facile componi tenerive potuerunt.   Notarium
voco et die admisso, quae formaveram dicto.   Abit
rursusque revocatur rursusque remittitur.

*At about 10 or 11 o'clock he retreats to the terrace or
covered portico for further reflection on his work.   After that
he goes for a ride in his carriage, returns for a rest, then takes
a walk.   Greek or Latin recitation follows (for the sake
of strengthening the digestion!), then another walk, an
anointing, a bath and supper.   Music or rest and conversation with the household members round off the day.*

Ubi hora quarta vel quinta (neque enim certum
15 dimensumque tempus), ut dies suasit, in xystum me
vel cryptoporticum confero, reliqua meditor et dicto.
Vehiculum ascendo.   Ibi quoque idem quod ambulans

aut iacens; durat intentio mutatione ipsa refecta.
Paulum redormio, dein ambulo, mox orationem
Graecam Latinamve clare et intente non tam vocis 20
causa quam stomachi lego; pariter tamen et illa
firmatur. Iterum ambulo, ungor, exerceor, lavor.
Cenanti mihi, si cum uxore vel paucis, liber legitur;
post cenam comoedus aut lyristes; mox cum meis
ambulo, quorum in numero sunt eruditi. Ita variis 25
sermonibus vespera extenditur, et quamquam longissimus dies cito conditur.

*Occasionally he varies this routine by riding on horseback,
receiving visitors from the neighbouring towns and going
hunting, the last always with his writing tablets. He allots
some time to his tenants.*

Non numquam ex hoc ordine aliqua mutantur.
Nam, si diu iacui vel ambulavi, post somnum demum
lectionemque non vehiculo sed, quod brevius quia 30
velocius, equo gestor. Interveniunt amici ex proxi-
mis oppidis partemque diei ad se trahunt inter-
dumque lassato mihi opportuna interpellatione
subveniunt. Venor aliquando, sed non sine pugillaribus, ut, quamvis nihil ceperim, non nihil referam. 35
Datur et colonis, ut videtur ipsis, non satis temporis,
quorum mihi agrestes querelae litteras nostras et haec
urbana opera commendant. Vale.

IX, 36

VI

*In winter, Pliny retired to his country house at Laurentum.
In this letter he describes minor changes in routine to allow
for increased business at the law courts.*

Scribis pergratas tibi fuisse litteras meas, quibus cognovisti quem ad modum in Tuscis otium aestatis exigerem; requiris quid ex hoc in Laurentino hieme permutem. Nihil, nisi quod meridianus somnus
5 eximitur, multumque de nocte vel ante vel post diem sumitur, et si agendi necessitas instat, quae frequens hieme, non iam comoedo vel lyristae post cenam locus, sed illa quae dictavi identidem retractantur, ac simul memoriae frequenti emendatione proficitur.

10 Habes aestate, hieme consuetudinem; nunc addas huc licet ver et autumnum, quae inter hiemem aestatemque media, ut nihil de die perdunt, ita de nocte parvulum acquirunt.   Vale.

IX, xl

THE HOUSEHOLDER

VII

This is a brief extract from a long letter in which Pliny extols the virtues of his house at Laurentum.   It is spacious without being too costly to maintain.   There is a simple entrance hall and a D-shaped portico, a pleasing inner hall and a dining hall which faces the sea.   There are many windows in the dining hall from which there are fine views.

Villa usibus capax, non sumptuosa tutela.   Cuius in prima parte atrium frugi nec tamen sordidum, deinde porticus in D litterae similitudine circumactae, quibus parvula sed festiva area includitur.   Egregium
5 hae adversus tempestates receptaculum;   nam specularibus ac multo magis imminentibus tectis muniuntur.   Est contra medias cavaedium hilare,

mox triclinium satis pulchrum, quod in litus excurrit
ac, si quando Africo mare impulsum est, fractis iam
et novissimis fluctibus leviter adluitur. Undique 10
valvas aut fenestras non minores valvis habet atque
ita a lateribus et a fronte quasi tria maria prospec-
tat; a tergo cavaedium, porticum, aream, porticum
rursus, mox atrium, silvas et longinquos respicit
montes. 15

*To the left of these buildings and lying back a little is a
large drawing room, and then a smaller room which has a
view of the sea. This is sheltered in winter and serves as a
gymnasium for his household. Only in bad weather is this
room useless.*

Huius a laeva retractius paulo cubiculum est
amplum, deinde aliud minus, quod altera fenestra
admittit orientem, occidentem altera retinet, hae et
subiacens mare longius, quidem, sed securius intuetur.
Huius cubiculi et triclinii illius obiectu includitur 20
angulus qui purissimum solem continet et accendit.
Hoc hibernaculum, hoc etiam gymnasium meorum
est; ibi omnes silent venti exceptis qui nubilum
inducunt et serenum ante quam usum loci eripiunt.

II, 17

THE EDUCATIONALIST

VIII

*Pliny wishes to see a school established in his native town,
Novum Comum. At present, the inhabitants of Novum
Comum are sending their children away to Milan for their
education. Pliny suggests that money now spent on*

*travelling and lodgings would be saved if a school could be
established at Comum. This letter is addressed to the
historian Tacitus.*

Salvum te in urbem venisse gaudeo; venisti autem,
si quando alias, nunc maxime mihi desideratus.   Ipse
pauculis adhuc diebus in Tusculano commorabor,
ut opusculum quod est in manibus absolvam.   Vereor
5 enim, ne, si hanc intentionem iam in finem laxavero,
aegre resumam.   Interim, ne quid festinationi meae
pereat, quod sum praesens petiturus, hac quasi
praecursoria epistula rogo.   Sed prius accipe causas
rogandi, deinde ipsum quod peto.
10   Proxime cum in patria mea fui, venit ad me
salutandum municipis mei filius praetextatus.   Huic
ego 'Studes?' inquam.   Respondit 'Etiam'.   'Ubi?'
'Mediolani'.   'Cur non hic?'   Et pater eius (erat
enim una atque etiam ipse adduxerat puerum):
15 'Quia nullos hic praeceptores habemus'.   'Quare
nullos?   Nam vehementer interest vestra, qui patres
estis' (et opportune complures patres audiebant),
'liberos vestros hic potissimum discere.   Ubi enim
aut iucundius morarentur quam in patria aut
20 pudicius continerentur quam sub oculis parentum
aut minore sumptu quam domi?

*He proposes that suitable teachers should be procured and
offers himself to contribute one third of the expense incurred.*

Quantulum est ergo collata pecunia conducere
praeceptores, quodque nunc in habitationes, in
viatica, in ea quae peregre emuntur (omnia autem
25 peregre emuntur), impenditis, adicere mercedibus?
Atque adeo ego, qui nondum liberos habeo, paratus

sum pro republica nostra, quasi pro filia vel parente,
tertiam partem eius quod conferre vobis placebit dare.
Totum etiam pollicerer, nisi timerem ne hoc munus
meum quandoque ambitu corrumperetur, ut accidere 30
multis in locis video, in quibus praeceptores publice
conducuntur. Huic vitio uno remedio occurri potest,
si parentibus solis ius conducendi relinquatur,
iisdemque religio recte iudicandi necessitate colla-
tionis addatur. Nam, qui fortasse de alieno negle- 35
gentes, certe de suo diligentes erunt, dabuntque
operam ne a me pecuniam nisi dignus accipiat, si
accepturus et ab ipsis erit.

Proinde consentite, conspirate maioremque animum
ex meo sumite, qui cupio esse quam plurimum quod 40
debeam conferre. Nihil honestius praestare liberis
vestris, nihil gratius patriae potestis. Educentur hic
qui hic nascuntur, statimque ab infantia natale solum
amare, frequentare consuescant. Atque utinam tam
claros praeceptores inducatis, ut finitimis oppidis 45
studia hinc petantur, utque nunc liberi vestri aliena
in loca ita mox alieni in hunc locum confluant!'

IV, 13

IX

*Although Pliny had no children, he had strong views on the
education of the young. In this letter he relates how he
reproved a father for being too severe towards his extravagant
son.*

Castigabat quidam filium suum quod paulo
sumptuosius equos et canes emeret. Huic ego,
iuvene digresso, 'heus tu, numquamne fecisti quod a
patre corripi posset? Fecisti, dico, non interdum

5 facis quod filius tuus, si repente pater ille, tu filius,
pari gravitate reprehendat? Non omnes homines
aliquo errore ducuntur? Non hic in illo sibi, in hoc
alius indulget?

Haec tibi admonitus immodicae severitatis exemplo
10 pro amore mutuo scripsi, ne quando tu quoque filium
tuum acerbius duriusque tractares. Cogita et illum
puerum esse et te fuisse, atque ita hoc quod es pater
utere, ut memineris et hominem esse te et hominis
patrem. Vale.

IX, 12

PLINY PUTS HUNTING IN ITS PLACE

X

*Someone who takes writing materials to a hunt cannot be
accused of wild enthusiasm for sport. This letter and the
next, which mildly attacks spectators at horse racing, reveals
Pliny's reservations about the 'sporting' life.*

Ridebis, et licet rideas. Ego ille, quem nosti, apros
tres et quidem pulcherrimos cepi. 'Ipse?' inquis.
Ipse; non tamen ut omnino ab inertia mea et quiete
discederem. Ad retia sedebam; erat in proximo non
5 venabulum aut lancea, sed stilus et pugillares; medi-
tabar aliquid enotabamque ut, si manus vacuas,
plenas tamen ceras reportarem. Non est quod
contemnas hoc studendi genus; mirum est ut animus
agitatione motuque corporis excitetur; iam undique
10 silvae et solitudo ipsumque illud silentium quod
venationi datur magna cogitationis incitamenta sunt.
Proinde, cum venabere, licebit auctore me ut
panarium et lagunculam sic etiam pugillares feras;

experieris non Dianam magis montibus quam
Minervam inerrare. Vale.

15

I, 6

XI

Omne hoc tempus inter pugillares ac libellos
iucundissima quiete transmisi. 'Quem ad modum',
inquis, 'in urbe potuisti?' Circenses erant; quo

ROMAN WRITING MATERIALS. A sealed and addressed
letter is shown here together with two wax tablets, a trimming
knife and writing materials.

genere spectaculi ne levissime quidem teneor. Nihil
novum, nihil varium, nihil quod non semel spectasse 5
sufficiat. Quo magis miror tot milia virorum tam
pueriliter identidem cupere currentes equos, insistentes
curribus homines videre. Si tamen aut velocitate
equorum aut hominum arte traherentur, esset ratio
nonnulla; nunc favent panno, pannum amant, et si 10
in ipso cursu medioque certamine hic color illuc, ille

huc transferatur, studium favorque transibit, et
repente agitatores illos, equos illos quos procul
noscitant, quorum clamitant nomina, relinquent.

15 Tanta gratia, tanta auctoritas in una vilissima
tunica, mitto apud vulgus, quod vilius tunica, sed
apud quosdam graves homines; quos ego cum
recordor in re inani, frigida, adsidua tam insatia-
biliter desidere, capio aliquam voluptatem quod hac

20 voluptate non capior. Ac per hos dies libentissime
otium meum in litteris colloco quos alii ntiosissimis
occupationibus perdunt. Vale.

IX, 6

THE PHILOSOPHER

XII

*The following brief extract is taken from a letter of
sympathy to a friend on the death of C. Fannius, who died
when his history of the lives of those who had been put to
death or had been banished by the emperor Nero was still
incomplete. Pliny deplores the death of those engaged upon
immortal work.*

Mihi autem videtur acerba semper et immatura
mors eorum qui immortale aliquid parant. Nam
qui, voluptatibus dediti, quasi in diem vivunt,
vivendi causas cotidie finiunt; qui vero posteros
5 cogitant et memoriam sui operibus extendunt, his
nulla mors non repentina est, ut quae semper incho-
atum aliquid abrumpat.

V, 5

XIII

*Pliny's cheerful disposition and capacity for the enjoyment
of simple pleasures are shown in this letter to a friend with
similar tastes.*

Bene est mihi quia tibi bene est. Habes uxorem
tecum, habes filium; frueris mari, fontibus, viridibus,
agro, villa amoenissima. Neque enim dubito esse
amoenissimam, in qua se composuerat homo felicior,
ante quam felicissimus fieret. Ego in Tuscis et venor 5
et studeo, quae interdum alternis, interdum simul
facio, nec tamen adhuc possum pronuntiare utrum sit
difficilius capere aliquid an scribere. Vale. *V, 18*

THE DINER-OUT

XIV

*Pliny relates his misfortune in being asked out to dine with
a person who set meaner food before the less-respected guests,
a practice which he roundly condemns.*

Longum est altius repetere, nec refert quemadmodum acciderit ut homo minime familiaris cenarem
apud quendam, ut sibi videbatur, lautum et diligentem
ut mihi, sordidum simul et sumptuosum. Nam sibi
et paucis optima quaedam, ceteris vilia et minuta 5
ponebat. Vinum etiam parvulis lagunculis in tria
genera discripserat, non ut potestas eligendi, sed ne
ius esset recusandi, aliud sibi et nobis, aliud minoribus
amicis (nam gradatim amicos habet), aliud suis
nostrisque libertis. Animadvertit qui mihi proximus 10
recumbebat et an probarem interrogavit. Negavi.
'Tu ergo', inquit, 'quam consuetudinem sequeris?'
'Eadem omnibus pono; ad cenam enim, non ad
notam invito cunctisque rebus exaequo, quos mensa
et toro aequavi'. 'Etiamne libertos?' 'Etiam; con- 15
victores enim tunc, non libertos puto'. Et ille:
'Magno tibi constat'. 'Minime.' 'Qui fieri potest?'
'Quia scilicet liberti mei non idem quod ego bibunt,
sed idem ego quod liberti'.

If only one abstains from gluttony and the modern self-indulgence alternated with meanness, one need not be extravagant.

20 Et hercule, si gulae temperes, non est onerosum quo utaris ipse communicare cum pluribus. Illa ergo reprimenda, illa quasi in ordinem redigenda est, si sumptibus parcas, quibus aliquanto rectius tua continentia quam aliena contumelia consulas.

25 Quorsum haec? Ne tibi, optimae indolis iuveni, quorumdam in mensa luxuria specie frugalitatis imponat. Convenit autem amori in te meo, quotiens tale aliquid inciderit, sub exemplo praemonere quid debeas fugere. Igitur memento nihil magis esse
30 vitandum quam istam luxuriae et sordium novam societatem; quae cum sint turpissima discreta ac separata, turpius iunguntur. Vale.

II, 6

THE NATURALIST

XV

The source of the river Clitumnus is still a beauty spot, as it was in Pliny's time.

Vidistine aliquando Clitumnum fontem? Si nondum (et puto nondum; alioqui narrasses mihi), vide quem ego (paenitet tarditatis) proxime vidi.

Modicus collis adsurgit antiqua cupressu nemorosus
5 et opacus. Hunc subter fons exit et exprimitur pluribus venis, sed imparibus, eluctatusque, quem facit gurgitem lato gremio patescit purus et vitreus, ut numerare iactas stipes et relucentis calculos possis. Inde non loci devexitate, sed ipsa sui copia et quasi

pondere, impellitur fons adhuc et iam amplissimum 10
flumen atque etiam navium patiens, quas obvias
quoque et contrario nisu in diversa tendentes transmittit
et perfert, adeo validus ut illa qua properat ipse,
quamquam per solum planum, remis non adiuvetur,
idem aegerrime remis contisque superetur adversus. 15
Iucundum utrumque per iocum ludumque fluitantibus,
ut flexerint cursum, laborem otio, otium labore
variare.

*The banks of the stream are clad with trees which are
reflected in the clear water. Beside the stream is a temple and
small chapels. A bridge spans the stream, near which are
baths, an inn and country houses.*

Ripae fraxino multa, multa populo vestiuntur,
quas perspicuus amnis velut mersas viridi imagine 20
adnumerat. Rigor aquae certaverit nivibus, nec
color cedit. Adiacet templum priscum et religiosum.
Stat Clitumnus ipse amictus ornatusque praetexta.
Praesens numen atque etiam fatidicum indicant
sortes. Sparsa sunt circa sacella complura totidem- 25
que di. Sua cuique veneratio, suum nomen, quibusdam vero etiam fontes. Nam praeter illum quasi
parentem ceterorum sunt minores capite discreti; sed
flumini miscentur, quod ponte transmittitur. Is
terminus sacri profanique. In superiore parte navi- 30
gare tantum, infra etiam natare concessum. Balineum Hispellates, quibus illum locum divus Augustus
dono dedit, publice praebent, praebent et hospitium.
Nec desunt villae, quae secutae fluminis amoenitatem
margini insistunt.
35

*This place has all kinds of interest, for there are numerous
inscriptions in praise of the god who watches over this shrine.*

In summa nihil erit ex quo non capias voluptatem.
Nam studebis quoque; et leges multa multorum
omnibus columnis, omnibus parietibus inscripta,
quibus fons ille deusque celebrantur. Plura laudabis,
40 non nulla ridebis; quamquam tu vero, quae tua
humanitas, nulla ridebis. Vale.

VIII, 8

XVI

*Pliny relates a strange story about a dolphin off the coast
of Hippo in North Africa which allowed a boy to ride on its
back. In view of our modern knowledge about dolphins, the
story can by no means be discounted.*

Est in Africa Hipponensis colonia mari proxima;
adiacet navigabile stagnum; ex hoc in modum
fluminis aestuarium emergit, quod vice alterna, prout
aestus aut repressit aut impulit, nunc infertur mari,
5 nunc redditur stagno. Omnis hic aetas piscandi,
navigandi, atque etiam natandi studio tenetur,
maxime pueri, quos otium ludusque sollicitat. His
gloria et virtus altissime provehi; victor ille qui
longissime ut litus ita simul nantes reliquit. Hoc
10 certamine puer quidam audentior ceteris in ulteriora
tendebat. Delphinus occurrit et nunc praecedere
puerum, nunc sequi, nunc circumire, postremo subire,
deponere, iterum subire trepidantemque perferre
primum in altum, mox flectit ad litus redditque terrae
15 et aequalibus. Serpit per coloniam fama; concurrere omnes, ipsum puerum tamquam miraculum
adspicere, interrogare, audire, narrare.

At first the dolphin caused apprehension, but gradually its tame behaviour began to inspire trust and boys swam up to it and stroked it. Another dolphin joined the first, but only as a spectator.

Postero die obsident litus, prospectant mare, et si quid mari simile. Natant pueri; inter hos ille, sed cautius. Delphinus rursus ad tempus, rursus ad puerum [venit]. Fugit ille cum ceteris. Delphinus, quasi invitet et revocet, exilit, mergitur, variosque orbes implicat expeditque. Hoc altero die, hoc tertio, hoc pluribus, donec homines innutritos mari subiret timendi pudor: accedunt et adludunt et appellant, tangunt etiam pertrectantque praebentem. Crescit audacia experimento. Maxime puer qui primus expertus est adnatat natanti, insilit tergo, fertur referturque, agnosci se, amari putat, amat ipse; neuter timet, neuter timetur; huius fiducia, mansuetudo illius augetur. Nec non alii pueri dextra laevaque simul eunt hortantes monentesque. Ibat una (id quoque mirum) delphinus alius, tantum spectator et comes. Nihil enim simile faciebat aut patiebatur, sed alterum illum ducebat reducebatque, ut puerum ceteri pueri.

Stranger still, the dolphin would even come on to the shore, dry itself and roll back into the sea.

Incredibile, tam verum tamen quam priora, delphinum gestatorem collusoremque puerorum in terram quoque extrahi solitum harenisque siccatum, ubi incaluisset in mare revolvi.

The deputy governor saw fit to pour some ointment over it as it lay on the shore, and this caused it to retire for some days.

*When it returned, local magistrates came to witness the sight,
and the cost of their entertainment was too much for the
small community to bear. The place was also losing its
seclusion. The dolphin was accordingly killed.*

Constat Octavium Avitum, legatum proconsulis
in litus educto religione prava superfudisse unguentum, cuius illum novitatem odoremque in altum
refugisse nec nisi post multos dies visum languidum
45 et maestum, mox redditis viribus priorem lasciviam
et solita ministeria repetisse.

Confluebant ad spectaculum omnes magistratus,
quorum adventu et mora modica res publica novis
sumptibus atterebatur.   Postremo locus ipse quietem
50 suam secretumque perdebat.   Placuit occulte interfici ad quod coibatur.

*You will receive this sad story with pity.   The truth needs
no embellishment.*

Haec tu qua miseratione, qua copia deflebis, orna-
bis, attolles! Quamquam non est opus adfingas
aliquid aut adstruas; sufficit ne ea quae sunt vera
55 minuantur.   Vale.

IX, 33

PLINY, EYEWITNESS
OF THE ERUPTION OF VESUVIUS

XVII

*On the afternoon of August 24th, A.D. 79, the volcano
Vesuvius erupted with such force that the towns Pompeii and
Herculaneum were buried under a thick layer of volcanic*

matter. Pliny and his mother were at Misenum with his uncle who was in command of the fleet there. His uncle sailed out to rescue survivors.

Erat Miseni classemque imperio praesens regebat. Nonum Kal. Septembres hora fere septima mater mea indicat ei apparere nubem inusitata et magnitudine et specie. Usus ille sole, mox frigida, gustaverat iacens studebatque; poscit soleas, ascendit 5 locum ex quo maxime miraculum illud conspici poterat. Nubes, incertum procul intuentibus ex quo monte (Vesuvium fuisse postea cognitum est), oriebatur, cuius similitudinem et formam non alia magis arbor quam pinus expresserit. Nam longis- 10 simo velut trunco elata in altum quibusdam ramis diffundebatur, credo, quia recenti spiritu evecta, dein senescente eo destituta aut etiam pondere suo victa in latitudinem evanescebat, candida interdum, interdum sordida et maculosa, prout terram cineremve sustul- 15 erat.

The Elder Pliny made ready to go to the rescue of friends and asked his nephew if he wished to accompany him. Pliny replied that he preferred to study the work his uncle had set him. The Elder Pliny accordingly set sail, and soon volcanic ash and small stones rained down on his boat. The next extract describes the Elder Pliny's brave rescue attempt.

Properat illuc unde alii fugiunt, rectumque cursum, recta gubernacula in periculum tenet, adeo solutus metu ut omnes illius mali motus, omnes figuras, ut deprehenderat oculis, dictaret enotaretque. 20

Iam navibus cinis inciderat, quo propius accederet, calidior et densior, iam pumices etiam nigrique et

ambusti et fracti igne lapides, iam vadum subitum
ruinaque montis litora obstantia. Cunctatus paulum,
25 an retro flecteret, mox gubernatori ut ita faceret
monenti 'Fortes,' inquit, 'fortuna iuvat. Pomponian-
um pete!'

*Although many fires were blazing on Vesuvius, the Elder
Pliny said that these were merely fires lighted by the country
folk. He retired to rest and actually slept, snoring a little.
The rain of ash and stones grew thicker, so Pliny's uncle was
aroused, but the sea was too rough and the winds too high
for him to sail back to Misenum.*

Interim e Vesuvio monte pluribus locis latissimae
flammae altaque incendia relucebant, quorum fulgor
30 et claritas tenebris noctis excitabatur. Ille agrestium
trepidatione ignes relictos desertasque villas per
solitudinem ardere in remedium formidinis dictitabat.
Tum se quieti dedit et quievit verissimo quidem
somno. Nam meatus animae, qui illi propter
35 amplitudinem corporis gravior et sonantior erat, ab
iis qui limini observabantur audiebatur.
Iam dies alibi, illic nox omnibus noctibus nigrior
densiorque; quam tamen faces multae variaque
lumina solabantur. Placuit egredi in litus et e
40 proximo aspicere ecquid iam mare admitteret; quod
adhuc vastum et adversum permanebat.

*The Elder Pliny lay down on a disused sail and repeatedly
asked for cold water. When the smell of sulphur grew
stronger, he stood up, supported by two slaves, but immediately
collapsed. His body was found later in a position resembling
sleep more than death.*

Ibi super abiectum linteum recubans semel atque
iterum frigidam poposcit hausitque. Deinde flammae
flammarumque praenuntius odor sulfuris alios in
fugam vertunt, excitant illum. Innitens servulis 45
duobus assurrexit et statim concidit, ut ego colligo,
crassiore caligine spiritu obstructo clausoque stomacho,
qui illi natura invalidus et angustus et frequenter
interaestuans erat. Ubi dies redditus (is ab eo
quem novissime viderat tertius) corpus inventum 50
est integrum, illaesum opertumque ut fuerat
indutus; habitus corporis quiescenti quam defuncto
similior.

VI, 16

XVIII

*Pliny is requested by Tacitus, to whom the last letter was
also written, to give his personal experiences of the eruption.
He explains how the earthquake shocks gradually increased in
violence until he and his mother decided to leave their bed-
rooms and sit in the forecourt of the house. A Spanish
friend of Pliny's uncle reproved Pliny for reading at such a
time.*

Ais te adductum litteris, quas exigenti tibi de morte
avunculi mei scripsi, cupere cognoscere, quos ego
Miseni relictus (id enim ingressus abruperam) non
solum metus, verum etiam casus pertulerim.

'Quamquam animus meminisse horret,
Incipiam'.   5

Profecto avunculo ipse reliquum tempus studiis
(ideo enim remanseram) impendi: mox balineum,
cena, somnus inquietus et brevis. Praecesserat per

10 multos dies tremor terrae minus formidulosus, quia
Campaniae solitus; illa vero nocte ita invaluit ut non
moveri omnia sed everti crederentur.   Inrumpit in
cubiculum meum mater; surgebam invicem, si
quiesceret excitaturus.   Residimus in area domus,
15 quae mare a tectis modico spatio dividebat.   Dubito
constantiam vocare an imprudentiam debeam;
agebam enim duodevicensimum annum.   Posco
librum Titi Livii et quasi per otium lego atque
etiam, ut coeperam, excerpo.   Ecce amicus avunculi,
20 qui nuper ad eum ex Hispania venerat, ut me et
matrem sedentes, me vero etiam legentem videt,
illius patientiam, securitatem meam corripit. Nihilo
segnius ego intentus in librum.

*At 6 a.m. the light remained poor.   There was great
danger from tottering houses.   We decided to leave the town.
A crowd followed us.   We saw coaches running to and fro
as the tremors continued and the sea was sucked back, leaving
many creatures stranded on the shore.   Inland a black cloud
now and again gaped open to reveal long flames, like lightning
flashes, but much larger.*

Iam hora diei prima, et adhuc dubius et quasi
25 languidus dies.   Iam quassatis circumiacentibus
tectis, quamquam in aperto loco, angusto tamen,
magnus et certus ruinae metus.   Tum demum
excedere oppido visum.   Sequitur vulgus attonitum,
quodque in pavore simile prudentiae, alienum con-
30 silium suo praefert ingentique agmine abeuntes
premit et impellit.   Egressi tecta consistimus.   Multa
ibi miranda, multas formidines patimur.   Nam
vehicula, quae produci iusseramus, quamquam in
planissimo campo, in contrarias partes agebantur ac

ne lapidibus quidem fulta in eodem vestigio quiesce- 35
bant. Praeterea mare in se resorberi et tremore
terrae quasi repelli videbamus. Certe processerat
litus multaque animalia maris siccis arenis detinebat.
Ab altero latere nubes atra et horrenda ignei spiritus
tortis vibratisque discursibus rupta in longas flam- 40
marum figuras dehiscebat; fulgoribus illae et similes
et maiores erant.

*The Spanish friend again implored Pliny to escape, but
himself hurried off when Pliny and his mother decided to
await news of the Elder Pliny. Soon afterwards the cloud
dropped lower, and Pliny's mother advised flight. Ash
started falling. They turned aside to avoid being trampled
down by the crowd. It became pitch dark, and shrieks and
crying could be heard. Many thought that the end of the
world was at hand.*

Tum vero ille idem ex Hispania amicus acrius et
instantius 'Si frater', inquit, 'tuus, tuus avunculus
vivit, vult esse vos salvos: si periit, superstites voluit. 45
Proinde quid cessatis evadere?' Respondimus non
commissuros nos ut de salute eius incerti nostrae con-
suleremus. Non moratus ultra proripit se effusoque
cursu periculo aufertur. Nec multo post illa nubes
descendere in terras, operire maria; cinxerat Capreas 50
et absconderat, Miseni quod procurrit abstulerat.
Tum mater orare, hortari, iubere, quoquo modo
fugerem; posse enim iuvenem, se et annis et corpore
gravem bene morituram, si mihi causa mortis non
fuisset. Ego contra salvum me nisi una non futurum; 55
deinde manum eius amplexus addere gradum cogo;
paret aegre, incusatque se quod me moretur. Iam
cinis, adhuc tamen rarus. Respicio; densa caligo tergis

imminebat quae nos torrentis modo infusa terrae
60 sequebatur. 'Deflectamus', inquam, 'dum vide-
mus, ne in via strati comitantium turba in tenebris
obteramur'. Vix consedimus et nox, non quasi illunis
aut nubila, sed qualis in locis clausis lumine exstincto.
Audires ululatus feminarum, infantium quiritatus,
65 clamores virorum; alii parentes, alii liberos, alii
coniuges vocibus requirebant, vocibus noscitant; hi
suum casum, illi suorum miserebantur; erant qui metu
mortis mortem precarentur. Multi ad deos manus
tollere; plures nusquam jam deos ullos aeternamque
70 illam et novissimam noctem mundo interpretabantur.

*Others increased the general panic by false rumours.
Gradually it grew lighter. Then came more darkness and
more ash. Pliny and his mother repeatedly had to shake off
the falling ashes. Pliny might have boasted his bravery at
this time, had he not consoled himself with the belief that
the world was coming to an end.*

Nec defuerunt qui fictis mentitisque terroribus vera
pericula augerent. Aderant qui Miseni illud ruisse,
illud ardere falso, sed credentibus nuntiabant.
Paulum reluxit; quod non dies nobis, sed adventantis
75 ignis indicium videbatur. Et ignis quidem longius
substitit, tenebrae rursus, cinis rursus, multus et
gravis. Hunc identidem adsurgentes excutiebamus;
operti alioqui atque etiam oblisi pondere essemus.
Possem gloriari non gemitum mihi, non vocem parum
80 fortem in tantis periculis excidisse, nisi me cum
omnibus, omnia mecum perire misero, magno tamen
mortalitatis solacio credidissem.

At length, day returned and the sun even shone. Every-

thing was covered in a thick layer of cinders. Pliny and his mother returned to Misenum where they spent an anxious night, since the earthquake still continued and frenzied souls prophesied future evils. All the same, Pliny and his mother resolved to await news of his uncle.

Pliny ends by stating that his letter is not worthy of being considered as history. If it is not even worth a letter, Tacitus, who asked for one, should hold himself responsible.

Tandem illa caligo tenuata, quasi in fumum nebulamve decessit; mox dies verus, sol etiam effulsit, luridus tamen, qualis esse cum deficit solet. 85 Occursabant trepidantibus adhuc oculis mutata omnia altoque cinere tamquam nive obducta. Regressi Misenum, curatis utcunque corporibus, suspensam dubiamque noctem spe ac metu exegimus. Metus praevalebat; nam et tremor terrae perse- 90 verabat et plerique lymphati terrificis vaticinationibus et sua et aliena mala ludificabantur. Nobis tamen ne tunc quidem, quamquam et expertis periculum et exspectantibus, abeundi consilium donec de avunculo nuntius.   95

Haec nequaquam historia digna non scripturus leges et tibi, scilicet qui requisisti imputabis, si digna ne epistula quidem videbuntur. Vale.

VI, 20

PLINY AND THE SUPERNATURAL

XIX

It becomes obvious from the three ghost stories told below that Pliny places some belief in supernatural powers.

The first concerns Curtius Rufus, attending upon the newly-appointed governor of Africa, to whom the spirit

*protecting Africa is said to have appeared and to have made
certain predictions which came true.*

Et mihi discendi et tibi docendi facultatem otium
praebet. Igitur perquam velim scire esse phantasmata et habere propriam figuram numenque aliquod
putes, an inania et vana ex metu nostro imaginem
5 accipere.

Ego ut esse credam, in primis eo ducor quod audio
accidisse Curtio Rufo. Tenuis adhuc et obscurus
obtinenti Africam comes haeserat. Inclinato die
spatiabatur in porticu; offertur ei mulieris figura
10 humana grandior pulchriorque: perterrito Africam se
futurorum praenuntiam dixit; iturum enim Romam
honoresque gesturum atque etiam cum summo
imperio in eandem provinciam reversurum ibique
moriturum. Facta sunt omnia. Praeterea acce-
15 denti Carthaginem egredientique nave eadem figura
in litore occurrisse narratur. Ipse certe implicitus
morbo futura praeteritis, adversa secundis auguratus
spem salutis, nullo suorum desperante, proiecit.

*The second story concerns a haunted house in Athens. The
ghost of an old man used to appear, accompanied by the
clanging of iron. The house was abandoned to the ghost, but
a poster was displayed to announce that it was for sale or lease.*

Erat Athenis spatiosa et capax domus, sed infamis
20 et pestilens. Per silentium noctis sonus ferri et, si
attenderes acrius, strepitus vinculorum longius primo,
deinde e proximo reddebatur. Mox apparebat
idolon, senex macie et squalore confectus, promissa
barba, horrenti capillo; cruribus compedes, manibus
25 catenas gerebat quatiebatque. Inde inhabitantibus

tristes diraeque noctes per metum vigilabantur;
vigiliam morbus et crescente formidine mors sequebatur; Nam interdiu quoque, quamquam abscess-
erat imago, memoria imaginis oculis inerrabat,
longiorque causis timoris timor erat. Deserta inde 30
et damnata solitudine domus totaque illi monstro
relicta; proscribebatur tamen, seu quis emere seu
quis conducere ignarus tanti mali vellet.

Athenodorus, a philosopher, came to Athens and, in spite
of suspecting its cheapness, took over this house. He sat up
all night until the ghost appeared, rattling its chains and
motioning Athenodorus to follow it. Athenodorus took up
his lamp and followed into the courtyard where the ghost
suddenly disappeared.

Venit Athenas philosophus Athenodorus, legit
titulum auditoque pretio, quia suspecta vilitas, 35
percunctatus omnia docetur ac nihilo minus, immo
tanto magis conducit. Ubi coepit advesperascere,
iubet sterni sibi in prima domus parte, poscit pugillares, stilum, lumen; suos omnes in interiora dimittit,
ipse ad scribendum animum, oculos, manum intendit, 40
ne vacua mens audita simulacra et inanes sibi metus
fingeret. Initio, quale ubique, silentium noctis;
deinde concuti ferrum, vincula moveri; ille non
tollere oculos, non remittere stilum, sed obfirmare
animum auribusque praetendere. Tum crebrescere 45
fragor, adventare et iam ut in limine, iam ut intra
limen audiri; respicit, videt agnoscitque narratam
sibi effigiem. Stabat innuebatque digito similis
vocanti. Hic contra, ut paulum exspectaret manu
significat rursusque ceris et stilo incumbit. Illa 50
scribentis capiti catenis insonabat. Respicit rursus
idem quod prius innuentem nec moratus tollit lumen

et sequitur. Ibat illa lento gradu, quasi gravis
vinculis. Postquam deflexit in aream domus, repente
55 dilapsa deserit comitem.

Athenodorus marked the spot where the ghost had dis-
appeared with grass and leaves. The following day he
asked the magistrates to have the place dug up. Bones inter-
twined with chains were found. These were publicly buried
and thereafter the ghost was duly laid.

Desertus, herbas et folia concerpta signum loco
ponit. Postero die adit magistratus, monet ut illum
locum effodi iubeant. Inveniuntur ossa inserta catenis
et implicita, quae corpus aevo terraque putrefactum
60 nuda et exesa reliquerat vinculis. Collecta publice
sepeliuntur. Domus postea rite conditis manibus
caruit.

Pliny himself vouches for the truth of the third story. One
of his freed men thought that he saw someone with a pair of
shears in his hand cutting off the hair of his brother Marcus,
another of Pliny's freed men. Hair was found on the floor
next morning. A similar event happened again a little later.
Pliny rather ingeniously attributes these happenings to the
fact that he escaped being prosecuted by Domitian after
being informed against by a certain Carus.

He concludes by asking his correspondent to give deep
consideration to the possibility that there are ghosts and then
to reach a firm decision, one way or the other, in order to
dispel Pliny's uncertainty.

Est libertus mihi Marcus, non illiteratus. Cum
hoc minor frater eodem lecto quiescebat. Is visus est
65 sibi cernere quendam in toro residentem admoventem-
que capiti suo cultros atque etiam ex ipso vertice

amputantem capillos. Ubi illuxit, ipse circa verticem
tonsus, capilli iacentes reperiuntur. Exiguum temporis
medium, et rursus simile aliud priori fidem fecit.
Puer in paedagogio mixtus pluribus dormiebat; 70
venerunt per fenestras (ita narrat) in tunicis albis
duo, cubantemque detonderunt et, qua venerant,
recesserunt. Hunc quoque tonsum sparsosque circa
capillos dies ostendit. Nihil notabile secutum, nisi
forte quod non fui reus; futurus, si Domitianus, 75
sub quo haec acciderunt, diutius vixisset. Nam in
scrinio eius datus a Caro de me libellus inventus est;
ex quo coniectari potest, quia reis moris est submittere capillum, recisos meorum capillos depulsi, quod
imminebat, periculi signum fuisse. 80

Proinde rogo eruditionem tuam intendas. Digna
res est, quam diu multumque consideres, ne ego
quidem indignus, cui copiam scientiae tuae facias.
Licet etiam utramque in partem, ut soles, disputes,
ex altera tamen fortius, ne me suspensum incertumque 85
dimittas, cum mihi consulendi causa fuerit, ut
dubitare desinerem. Vale.

VII, 27

THE PROVINCIAL GOVERNOR

XX

*The last book of letters (Book X) illustrates the tasks that
Pliny undertook as provincial governor in Bithynia. Some
of these letters may be considered as pairs, when Pliny asks
the Emperor Trajan for guidance on some point and receives
a reply from him. The next two letters form such a pair:
in the first Pliny reports a fire which caused considerable
damage and asks that a guild of firemen be formed to
extinguish fires.*

Trajan replies that similar guilds have troubled the peace of Pliny's province. He therefore instructs Pliny to see to the provision of fire-fighting equipment and to direct householders themselves to take steps for the protection of their homes.

Cum diversam partem provinciae circumirem, Nicomediae vastissimum incendium multas privatorum domos et duo publica opera, quamquam via interiacente, Gerusian et Iseon, absumpsit. Est autem latius
5 sparsum primum violentia venti, deinde inertia hominum, quos satis constat otiosos et immobiles tanti mali spectatores perstitisse; et alioqui nullus usquam in publico sipho, nulla hama, nullum denique instrumentum ad incendia compescenda. Et haec
10 quidem, ut iam praecepi, parabuntur. Tu, domine, dispice, an instituendum putes collegium fabrorum dumtaxat hominum CL. Ego attendam ne quis nisi faber recipiatur, neve iure concesso in aliud utatur; nec erit difficile custodire tam paucos.

X, 33

XXI

Tibi quidem secundum exempla complurium in mentem venit posse collegium fabrorum apud Nicomedenses constitui. Sed meminerimus provinciam istam et praecipue eas civitates eius modi
5 factionibus esse vexatas. Quodcumque nomen ex quacumque causa dederimus iis qui in idem contracti fuerint, hetaeriae aeque brevi fient. Satius itaque est comparari ea quae ad coercendos ignes auxilio esse possint, admonerique dominos praediorum, ut et ipsi
10 inhibeant ac, si res poposcerit, accursu populi ad hoc uti.

X, 34

XXII

Pliny sends felicitations to Trajan on his birthday.

Opto, domine, et hunc natalem et plurimos alios
quam felicissimos agas aeternaque laude florentem
virtutis tuae gloriam et incolumis et fortis aliis super
alia operibus augeas.

X, 88

XXIII

*Treatment of early Christians is a very important subject
in the next two letters. Pliny admits lack of experience in
dealing with Christians, and asks whether consideration
should be given to the age of the Christian and if recantation
should bring pardon or whether the mere admission of
Christianity is punishable.*

Solemne est mihi, domine, omnia de quibus
dubito ad te referre. Quis enim potest melius vel
cunctationem meam regere vel ignorantiam instruere?
Cognitionibus de Christianis interfui numquam.
Ideo nescio quid et quatenus aut puniri soleat aut 5
quaeri. Nec mediocriter haesitavi sitne aliquod
discrimen aetatum, an quamlibet teneri nihil a
robustioribus differant, detur paenitentiae venia, an
ei qui omnino Christianus fuit desisse non prosit,
nomen ipsum, etiamsi flagitiis careat, an flagitia 10
cohaerentia nomini puniantur.

*For the time being Pliny has followed this method: he
asks suspects if they are Christians, then, if they confess, he
asks them twice again, threatening death. Those who*

*persevere in the same answer he leads out to be executed, on
the grounds that inflexible obstinacy should be punished.*

Interim in iis qui ad me tamquam Christiani
deferebantur hunc sum secutus modum. Interrogavi ipsos an essent Christiani. Confitentes iterum
15 ac tertio interrogavi supplicium minatus. Perse-
verantes duci iussi. Neque enim dubitabam, qualecunque esset quod faterentur, pertinaciam certe et
inflexibilem obstinationem debere puniri. Fuerunt
alii similis amentiae; quos, quia cives Romani erant,
20 adnotavi in urbem remittendos.

*As accusations spread, a notice is put up giving the names
of persons alleged to be Christians. This is unsigned.
Pliny orders these persons to be sought out and then con-
fronts them with an image of Trajan and bids them to
pay homage to it and to the gods and to curse Christ.
Their only crime, however, as far as he can ascertain, is
to hold meetings, sing hymns to Christ and to promise not to
commit sins. After this they separate and take food, quite
harmless food. In spite of using torture on two female slaves,
Pliny can discover no more than 'a depraved, excessive
superstition'.*

Mox ipso tractatu, ut fieri solet, diffundente se
crimine plures species inciderunt. Propositus est
libellus sine auctore multorum nomina continens.
Qui negabant se esse Christianos aut fuisse, cum
25 praeeunte me deos appellarent et imagini tuae, quam
propter hoc iusseram cum simulacris numinum adferri,
ture ac vino supplicarent, praeterea maledicerent
Christo, quorum nihil posse cogi dicuntur qui sunt
re vera Christiani, dimittendos esse putavi. Alii ab

indice nominati esse se Christianos dixerunt et mox 30
negaverunt; fuisse quidem, sed desiisse, quidam ante
triennium, quidam ante plures annos, non nemo
etiam ante viginti quinque. Omnes et imaginem
tuam deorumque simulacra venerati sunt: et Christo
maledixerunt.
                                                    35

Adfirmabant autem hanc fuisse summam vel culpae
suae vel erroris quod essent soliti stato die ante lucem
convenire carmenque Christo quasi deo dicere secum
invicem, seque sacramento non in scelus aliquod
obstringere, sed ne furta, ne latrocinia, ne adulteria 40
committerent, ne fidem fallerent, ne depositum
appellati abnegarent. Quibus peractis morem sibi
discedendi fuisse rursusque coeundi ad capiendum
cibum, promiscuum tamen et innoxium; quod ipsum
facere desiisse post edictum meum, quo secundum 45
mandata tua hetaerias esse vetueram. Quo magis
necessarium credidi ex duabus ancillis quae ministrae
dicebantur quid esset veri et per tormenta quaerere.
Sed nihil aliud inveni quam superstitionem pravam,
immodicam.
                                                    50

Pliny has consulted Trajan because a large number of
people are involved. The contagion has spread from the
cities to the countryside. Yet the temples are now being
frequented again and sacred festivals are being revived, so
that many may be reclaimed from Christianity if they are
offered the chance of repenting.

Ideo dilata cognitione ad consulendum te decurri.
Visa est enim mihi res digna consultatione, maxime
propter periclitantium numerum. Multi enim omnis
aetatis, omnis ordinis, utriusque sexus etiam, vocantur
in periculum et vocabuntur. Neque enim civitates 55

tantum, sed vicos etiam atque agros superstitionis
istius contagio pervagata est; quae videtur sisti et
corrigi posse.   Certe satis constat, prope iam desolata
templa coepisse celebrari, et sacra solemnia diu
60 intermissa repeti: passimque venire victimas, quarum
adhuc rarissimus emptor inveniebatur.   Ex quo facile
est opinari quae turba hominum emendari possit, si
fiat paenitentiae locus.

X, 96

XXIV

*The Emperor Trajan replies in a vein moderate for the
times.   No hard and fast rules can be applied.   The guilty
must be punished, but repentance gains full pardon.   Unsigned information is inadmissible as evidence against
anyone, for acceptance of such information would start a
precedent both very evil and contrary to the spirit of the times.*

Actum quem debuisti, mi Secunde, in excutiendis
causis eorum qui Christiani ad te delati fuerant, secutus
es.   Neque enim in universum aliquid quod quasi
certam formam habeat constitui potest.   Conquirendi
5 non sunt; si deferantur et arguantur, puniendi sunt, ita
tamen ut qui negaverit se Christianum esse idque
re ipsa manifestum fecerit, id est supplicando diis
nostris, quamvis suspectus in praeteritum fuerit,
veniam ex paenitentia impetret.   Sine auctore vero
10 propositi libelli nullo crimine locum habere debent.
Nam et pessimi exempli, nec nostri saeculi est.

X, 97

NOTES

I

1. **C. Plinius Secundus Septicio Suo S.:** Pliny used this familiar Roman method for starting most of his letters. The *S* is short for *salutem dat*='gives greeting to'. The whole heading therefore means 'Caius Plinius Secundus (gives greeting) to his (friend) Septicius'. *Caius* is a common praenomen, or personal name. *Plinius* is the name of his uncle which he assumed when his uncle adopted him. **Caecilius,** which appears in his full name, is that of his family or *gens*, corresponding to our surname. **Secundus,** 'the second', was used to distinguish him from his uncle.

si quas paulo accuratius scripsissem: The comparative *accuratius* is difficult to represent in translation. Say, 'If I have written any letters having some degree of polish'.

3. **scripsissem:** This is virtually indirect speech. Pliny's friend would have said 'if you have written=*si scripsisti*': Pliny reports the idea in the past; hence the pluperfect subjunctive of indirect speech.

4. **non servato temporis ordine:** Say 'without keeping to the order in which they were written'.

5. **quaeque** (*epistula*): is the subject of **venerat.**

6. **superest ut:** 'it remains that'. **te consilii paeniteat:** 'that you may repent of your plan'. Impersonal verbs of 'feeling', such as *me miseret*: I pity, *me taedet*: I am tired, *me pudet*: I am ashamed, *me piget*: I hate, are followed as here, *te paeniteat*, by a genitive of 'further object'.

7. **flet:** Examine carefully the tense.

II

1. **In causa amor primum:** Translate 'Love is the main reason'. **consuevimus:** 'we are accustomed'. The perfect

39

of -*sco* verbs has a present meaning: e.g. we have been accustomed—therefore we are accustomed.

7. **similis excluso:** A common term in the language of lovers. Translate 'like an excluded lover'.

8. **in foro et amicorum litibus:** Pliny explains that the only time he does not miss his wife is when he is fully occupied in court.

     (*a*)   (*b*)   (*b*)   (*a*)

10. **requies in labore, in miseria curisque solacium:** Pliny is fond of using the figure of speech known as chiasmus, derived from the Greek letter chi (χ). This involves placing two sets of words that have to be contrasted in the order *a b*, *b a*. Here *requies* corresponds with *solacium* and *in labore* with *in miseria*. The natural order would be *requies in labore, solacium in miseria curisque* (*ab*, *ab*), but the use of chiasmus embellishes his style.

III

2. **libellos,** here = *epistulas*.

3. **in vestigio meo:** Translate 'in a place where I used to be'. Account for the moods of **teneas** and **colloces**.

4. **quod his fomentis adquiescis:** 'that you find consolation in these comforts'.

5. **lectito:** like *dictito*, and others is a frequentitive verb which implies repeated action.

6. **novas:** refers to **epistulas**, not to **manus**.

7. **tui:** objective genitive.

8. **suavitatis:** partitive genitive after **tantum**. Again, **dulcedinis** is partitive genitive after **quantum**.

9. **licet hoc ita me delectet ut torqueat:** lit. 'although this so delights me as to torture me'. Try to express a little more freely in good English.

10. **delectet:** Note that **licet** may be followed by the subjunctive without any 'warning' *ut*. **torqueat:** Explain the mood.

V

odel of tender regard'.

... .ʲᵉᶜᵗⁱᵛᵉ ᵍᵉⁿⁱᵗⁱᵛᵉ after **amantissimum.**

3. **ut:** 'as'. **patris amissi adfectum:** 'the affection of a lost father'. Calpurnia had lost her father when young. It is possible that she lost her mother as well, which would account for the fact that Hispulla, her aunt, looked after her.

4. **repraesentes:** originally meant 'to bring back', 'pay back'; here simply 'show'.

6. **evadere:** sc. *illam* as the accusative of the Acc. + infin. construction.

10. **cum videor acturus:** 'when I am about to plead a cause.' As explained later in this letter, Calpurnia often listened to Pliny in court.

12. **qui nuntient:** What does *qui* with subjunctive express?

14. **in proximo:** 'close by'. *Proximo* preceded by prepositions is quite common in Pliny.

16. **formatque cithara:** we should say 'and sets them *to* the lyre'.

21. **aetatem meam aut corpus:** Pliny was already middle-aged when he married Calpurnia.

22. **Nec aliud decet tuis manibus educatam:** lit. 'Nor otherwise does beseem one raised by your hands'. Translate 'Nor would any other quality seem right in one trained by your hands'.

24. **contubernio:** Primarily a military word, denoting the companionship of those who shared a tent. Post-Augustan writers use it a more general sense. Perhaps 'under your roof' conveys best the meaning here.

29. **gratias ago** + dat.: the usual way of saying 'I thank'.

31. **invicem elegeris:** 'you have chosen in turn', i.e. her (Calpurnia) for him (Pliny) and him for her.

V

1. **in Tuscis:** 'in my Tuscan country house'. This was situated on the higher reaches of the Tiber, near the town of Tifernum. This was his summer resort. In winter he stayed at Laurentum.

3. **circa horam primam:** The first hour for Romans started at daybreak.

4. **saepe ante, tardius raro:** Observe the chiasmus (*a b, b a*).

5. **ab iis quae avocant:** 'from those factors which distract'.

6. **non oculos animo sed animum oculis sequor:** Pliny enjoys playing with the order of words in this manner, affording another example of chiasmus.

8. **quotiens non vident alia:** 'whenever they do not see other distractions'.

9. **ad verbum scribenti . . . similis:** 'like one writing the exact wording'. Pliny explains that he prepares mentally word for word what he intends to write.

15. **dies:** here means 'weather'.

18. **durat intentio mutatione ipsa refecta:** 'my concentration lasts, refreshed by the very change (of scenery)'.

22. **ungor, exercèor, lavòr:** Latin writers sometimes use the passive to convey the Greek 'middle' voice which often has a reflexive sense. Translate: 'I anoint myself, take exercise and bathe'.

24. **cum meis ambulo:** sc. *libertis*, i.e. *cum meis libertis ambulo*.

26. **et quamquam longissimus dies:** Translate *quamquam* here as 'even': 'and even the longest day'.

34. **Venor aliquando, sed non sine pugillaribus:** In letter I, 6 (extract X in this selection), Pliny explains that he was in the habit of taking his writing materials to the hunt.

36. **ut videtur ipsis:** translate 'as it seems to them' or 'as they think'.

37. **quorum mihi agrestes querelae:** Doubtless, these rustic complaints caused Pliny some annoyance. By comparison they gave Pliny's letter writing and city business considerable attraction.

38. **haec urbana opera:** 'this city business'.

 commendant: 'make more attractive'.

VI

3. **quid ex hoc . . . permutem:** 'what alteration from this routine'.

5. **multumque de nocte vel ante vel post diem sumitur:** All that Pliny is stating is that he sleeps less.

6. **si agendi necessitas instat:** 'if the pressure of the law courts is impending'. As Pliny goes on to explain, there was more forensic work to attend to in the winter than in the summer months.

8. **identidem retractantur . . . memoriae frequenti emendatione proficitur:** Pliny believed in painstaking revision, correction or memorisation of his work.

10. **addas licet:** 'you may add'.

11. **quae . . . media . . . perdunt:** 'which . . . coming between . . . lose . . .'.

12. **ut . . . ita:** 'while . . . so'.

VII

1. **Villa usibus capax: non sumptuosa tutela:** Pliny frequently writes sentences that lack verbs. Often, as here, part of the verb 'to be' has to be supplied to complete the sense. *usibus capax*: large enough for a variety of uses'. *tutela*: This is ablative of description. Translate 'not expensive in *upkeep*'.

2. **atrium frugi nec tamen sordidum:** Pliny explains that this hall is not shabby, but does not rival the more ostentatious *atria* of his time. The *atrium* in most Roman houses was the equivalent to our 'living room'.

3. **porticus:** Note that this word is plural. A kind of double portico shaped like two capital letter D's back to back (Dꓷ) is therefore indicated.

7. **medias:** supply '*porticus*'.

8. **mox:** as often in Pliny = 'next'.

triclinium: The *triclinium*, so called from the three couches placed along three of its walls, was equivalent to our dining room. The Romans ate, reclining on one elbow, from a centrally placed table.

9. **Africo:** supply '*vento*'.

13. **a tergo:** i.e. if you turn round completely and look back towards the entrance.

14. **silvas et . . . montes:** Some of this countryside is still well wooded. The 'mountains' would be the Alban Hills.

16. **cubiculum:** This does not always mean bedroom. It is a general term for any room. This room would serve as a drawing room.

20. **Huius cubiculi . . . accendit:** Translate 'From the siting of this drawing room and the dining room just mentioned an angle is enclosed which holds and increases the sun at its height'.

22. **hibernaculum:** This was, in fact, Pliny's winter retreat.

meorum: this word refers to his household of slaves and freedmen.

23. **exceptis qui:** 'with the exception of those winds which' . . . The point is that only dull weather makes this room unpleasant to use.

24. **serenum eripiunt ante quam usum loci:** is perhaps an easier order to grasp.

VIII

2. **si quando alias: nunc maxime desideratus:** *desideratus* goes with both phrases.

3. **pauculis adhuc diebus:** 'for a few days yet'.

   in Tusculano: 'on my Tusculum estate'. This was some 17 miles from Rome to the south-east, in the Alban Hills area.

6–8. **ne quid festinationi meae pereat, quod sum praesens petiturus, hac quasi praecursoria epistula rogo:** 'lest any time may be lost—since I am in a hurry—I am asking in this, so to speak, precursory letter what I shall be asking you in person'.

10. **in patria mea:** Here *patria* is used for 'home town'.

11. **praetextatus:** The *toga praetexta* was worn by freeborn Roman citizens up to the age of about sixteen. It was white with a purple stripe at the border. When a child reached 16, he underwent a ceremony of discarding the *toga praetexta* and the *bulla* (or locket) and assumed the pure white *toga virilis*, but higher magistrates wore a *toga praetexta*.

12. **Etiam:** 'Yes'. An alternative for *ita vero, certe*, equivalent to a short affirmative reply.

13. **Mediolani:** What case is this? Milan, both in Pliny's time and now, is the most important city in Northern Italy. Its educational facilities were very good and it was called '*Novae Athenae*'.

15. **praeceptores:** (acc.) equivalent to *magistros*, a general word for non-specialist teachers.

16. **interest vestra:** 'it concerns you'. *Interest* is followed by the genitive of the noun: e.g. *regis interest*, but the ablative of the possessive adjectives: *mea, tua, nostra* and *vestra*.

22. **quantulum est:** 'What a simple matter it would be'.

24. **viatica:** travelling expenses.

25. **mercedibus:** this word means not only fees but also, as here, salaries.

26. **qui nondum liberos habeo:** Pliny was disappointed in his desire to have a family. This letter was written shortly after he married Calpurnia.

27. **republica . . . filia . . . parente:** all illustrate Pliny's love of Comum.

30. **ambitu corrumperetur:** Pliny's belief was that the townsmen should share the cost of providing teachers. In this way, since they would all have a personal stake in the school, there would be less chance of graft.

32. **Huic vitio** (*dat.*) **uno remedio** (*abl.*) **occurri** (*pass. inf.*): Translate 'This fault can be relieved by one remedy'.

34. **religio recte iudicandi:** *Religio* seldom means religion. 'The *duty* of judging correctly' would suit the sense here.

40. **ex meo:** *animo* is understood.

42. **educentur:** What kind of subjunctive is this?

44. **consuescant:** the same subjunctive as that above.

44. **utinam:** This word introduces a wish for the future which is expressed by the present subjunctive **inducatis.** Why are **petantur** and **confluant** in the subjunctive?

IX

3. **iuvene digresso:** Observe Pliny's tact in not reproving the father in front of his son. The word 'said' has to be supplied before the direct speech. **heus tu:** quite a strong ejaculation: 'look here, man'.

5. **si repente pater ille, tu filius:** The verbs are omitted. Imagine that the sentence reads '*Si repente pater esset ille, tu esses filius.*'

7. **Non hic in illo sibi, in hoc alius indulget:** Observe the

balancing of the two parts of the sentence. In translating,
it will help to take *indulget* into the first half of the sentence.

9. **Haec tibi admonitus immodicae severitatis exemplo
pro amore mutuo scripsi:** The order may be simplified
as follows: *admonitus exemplo immodicae severitatis haec tibi
scripsi pro mutuo amore.*

11. **acerbius duriusque:** '*too* harshly and *too* severely'.

13. **utere:** What part of the verb is this?

X

2. **et quidem:** *et eos* would be more normal in Augustan
prose.

3. **ab inertia mea et quiete discederem:** Pliny refers with
some diffidence to his literary activities. Practical Romans
tended to regard literary pursuits as '*inertia*'.

4. **in proximo:** 'close at hand'.

5. **pugillares:** 'wax tablets', derived from the word
pugillus = a handful. These tablets could be held in the
hand and were the equivalent of our notebooks.

7. **Non est quod:** 'There is no reason why'.

8. **ut:** how.

12. **venabere** = *venaberis*. **auctore me:** 'on my advice'.

14. **Dianam:** Diana was identified with the Greek goddess
Artemis, the virgin goddess of hunting, as well as goddess
of the moon.

15. **Minervam:** The Roman equivalent of Pallas Athene.
Minerva was the goddess of learning. Pliny makes the
point that, even when hunting, he finds time for his writing.

XI

3. **Circenses:** The Circensian games were held every year
at Rome in September. The races took place in the Circus
Maximus, which had been twice damaged by fires in the

reigns of Nero and Domitian, but had been freshly restored by Trajan at the time Pliny writes. The Horse-racing was managed by companies (*factiones*). Originally, in Republican days, there were only two companies, the Red (*russata*) and the White (*albata*), but the Green (*prasina*) and Blue (*veneta*) were soon added, while in Domitian's day and after the Gold (*aurata*) and Purple (*purpurata*) made a total of six teams.

4. **Nihil novum, nihil varium, nihil quod non semel spectasse sufficiat:** It may be that Pliny is deliberately imitating Cicero's views on such games: *Quae tamen si videnda sunt, saepe vidisti, neque nos qui spectavimus quidquam novi vidimus.* Note the alliteration in *semel spectasse sufficiat*.

7. **currentes equos:** Usually four chariots ran in each race.

10. **panno:** lit. a patch. Pliny has chosen this word to show his contempt for racing. Like our modern jockeys, the Roman riders would wear their team colours.

12. **studium favorque:** the enthusiasm and support of the spectators. **transibit:** note that we might have expected a present subjunctive here to correspond with the protasis (*si* clause) verb **transferatur.** Pliny uses the future indicative to make the meaning more graphic.

16. **mitto apud vulgus:** 'I pass over its influence over the common people'. Pliny, like Horace—*Odi profanum vulgus*—can be a prig at times. **quod vilius tunica:** He decidedly looks down upon the mob! Note that *tunica* is abl. of comparison.

17. **quos:** change into *et eos* and incorporate in acc. + infin. as follows: *et cum recordor eos desidere. . . .*

18. **frigida:** 'tame', 'lacking in interest'.

XII

3. **quasi in diem vivunt:** 'live, as it were, for the present hour'.

4. **vivendi causas cotidie finiunt:** 'daily put an end to

their purpose of living'. **posteros cogitant:** 'reflect upon those to come after them'.

5. **sui:** objective genitive.

XIII

2. **viridibus:** a post-Augustan word, meaning 'greenery', 'green foliage'.

4. **amoenissimam:** sc. *villam.*

in qua se composuerat homo felicior, ante quam **felicissimus fieret:** This is rather difficult. Translation becomes easier if we take *felicior* as 'quite happy': 'in which a man had settled himself quite happily before he became the happiest man alive'.

6. **interdum alternis, interdum simul facio:** As we saw in an earlier letter (Extract X) Pliny sometimes attempted to hunt and write at the same time.

8. **capere aliquid:** i.e. to catch some game.

XIV

1. **Longum est altius repetere:** 'It would be tedious to dwell upon the matter too deeply'.

2. **homo minime familiaris:** this, of course, refers to Pliny himself. Translate: 'a man by no means interested in society'. It is possible, however, that *familiaris* may apply to this particular friendship.

4. **sordidum simul et sumptuosum:** Note the alliteration.

5. **minuta:** almost equivalent to our word 'scraps'.

9. **gradatim amicos habet:** 'he has his friends classed', i.e., his best friends received the best food.

10. **Animadvertit . . . interrogavit:** A simplified order would be: (*is*) *qui mihi proximus recumbebat animadvertit et interrogavit an probarem.*

11. **recumbebat:** The Romans did not sit up to their

main meals, but reclined, propped up on their elbows, on couches.

14. **notam:** the *nota censoria* was a mark that the Roman censors added to their citizen lists if a person was censured for any misdemeanour. Pliny makes the point that he invites his guests to a meal, not to be censured.

17. **magno tibi constat:** 'It costs you a good deal'.

20. **hercule:** Pliny uses this word for mild exclamations, equivalent to 'Good heavens!'

22. **quasi in ordinem redigenda est:** The expression '*in ordinem redigere*' means 'to reduce to the ranks'. The *quasi* softens the tone a little to mean 'brought into control'.

25. **Quorsum haec?:** 'What is the point of all this?'

29. **memento:** 'remember'. What part of the verb is this?

XV

1. **Clitumnum:** The river Clitumnus, a tributary of the Tinia, which itself runs into the Tiber, was and remains a famous beauty spot. Vergil mentioned the fine cattle that grazed on its banks: '*Hinc albi Clitumne greges*'. Suetonius mentioned that Caligula visited the place.

2. **alioqui narrasses:** 'otherwise you would have told me'. Understand a '*si vidisses*' to complete the whole conditional sentence.

3. **tarditatis:** a further genitive is usual after impersonal verbs of feeling: '*paenitet me tarditatis*' is the full expression.

5. **exprimitur:** lit. 'is squeezed out'. Translate 'bursts forth'.

6. **eluctatus:** 'having broken out'.

8. **stipes:** Here 'small coins'. The practice of throwing coins into fountains in Italy and elsewhere is quite common, e.g. the Fountain of the Trevi in Rome.

10. **impellitur fons adhuc et iam amplissimum flumen:** 'it is driven on, a fountain up to here and now a full-flowing river'. The transition from stream to river is swift and remarkable.

11. **etiam navium patiens . . . transmittit et perfert:** Pliny says that the river is capable of taking vessels, but that they have difficulty passing upstream against the current.

12–14. **adeo validus, ut illa qua properat ipse, quamquam per solum planum, remis non adiuvetur:** translate 'so strong (i.e. the river Clitumnus) that in that direction (*via* understood after *illa*) in which it hurries, although through level ground, (lit. it is not helped by oars) there is no need to row'.

17. **ut flexerint cursum:** Toiling against the river and lazily floating down it 'when they change course' makes for good sport.

laborem otio, otium labore variare: Note the chiasmus again.

23. **Clitumnus.** The chief god of Umbria was called Jupiter Clitumnus. This figure is standing and clothed, whereas most river gods were portrayed nude and reclining on one elbow.

28. **minores:** sc. *fontes*. **capite discreti:** lit 'separated in their springs'.

29. **quod ponte transmittitur:** 'which is crossed by a bridge'.

31. **infra etiam natare concessum:** The Romans often practised hygiene in the name of religion.

32. **Hispellates:** The town of Hispellum was some twelve miles downstream, the modern Spello. Inscriptions including the word '*Hispellates*' have been found here.

37. **et leges multa . . . inscripta:** We know well from the *graffiti* at Pompeii and from comments in Martial and other authors that scribbling on walls is not the prerogative of modern times.

XVI

1. **Hipponensis:** The town of Hippo was situated not far from Carthage.

2. **stagnum:** The word is used both for fresh water and salt water pools.

3 **aestuarium:** a channel which connected the pool with the sea, so that the pool would be full at high tide.

5. **Omnis aetas:** 'People of all ages'.

6. **His gloria:** supply *est.*

8. **victor ille:** again, supply *est.*

11. **praecedere, sequi** etc.: note that these are historic infinitives. The historic infinitive is the present infinitive used to stress vivid action in the past. Translate as *praecessit, secutus est.*

12. **subire:** 'came up from under', i.e. took the boy on its back.

15. **concurrere** etc.: again historic infinitives.

18. **et si quid mari simile:** i.e. the *stagnum* and the *aestuarium.*

26. **pertrectantque praebentem:** lit. 'and they stroked him offering', i.e. allowing himself to be stroked.

39. **extrahi:** middle use: 'was in the habit of coming out' (of the water). The Romans commonly believed that dolphins could not live out of water.

40. **revolvi:** also middle use: lit. rolling itself back.

42. **educto:** sc. *delphino.* **superfudisse unguentum:** This may have been a purification ceremony or, possibly an act of worship towards the miraculous dolphin.

48. **mora:** 'lengthy stay'. **modica res publica:** This small town could not afford lavish entertainment of visitors.

50. **secretum:** used as noun here, 'privacy'.

Placuit (supply *eis*) **occulte interfici ad quod coibatur:** 'They resolved that the object (dolphin) to which the crowds flocked should be killed'.

53. **adfingas . . . adstruas:** A rare use of *opus* with subj. without *ut*. Translate: 'Although you have no need to . . .'.

XVII

1. **Erat:** 'He was . . .' i.e. Pliny's uncle. **Miseni:** Misenum is at the north west end of the Bay of Naples. It was a station for a Roman fleet.

2. **Nonum Kal. Septembres:** The fateful day, August 24th, A.D. 79. **hora fere septima:** Midday was always the sixth hour.

4. **Usus ille sole, mox frigida:** 'He sunbathed and then had a bath'.

5. **poscit soleas:** The Romans removed their sandals when reclining at meals. When a guest or host asked for his sandals, it was understood that he was about to leave the house.

10. **pinus:** the Italian pine that Pliny has in mind spreads outwards, umbrella-shaped. The smoke of the eruption must have 'mushroomed' out like that of an atomic bomb.

12. **quia recenti . . . in latitudinem evanescebat:** 'because, carried up by a fresh gust, and then abandoned as the gust grew weak, or even overcome by its own weight, it began to dissolve laterally'.

19. **solutus metu:** 'freed from fear'.

26. **Pomponianus:** A friend of the Elder Pliny. Do not confuse with Pompeii.

34. **meatus animae:** 'his breathing'.

39. **Placuit egredi:** Supply '*ei*'.

40. **ecquid iam mare admitteret:** 'What the sea might now permit'. The Elder Pliny had sailed in on a following breeze, but the seas were still running high and inshore so threateningly that he could not put out again.

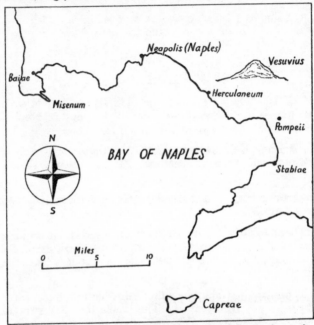

THE BAY OF NAPLES. This sketch map marks the main areas affected by the eruption of Vesuvius, A.D. 79, described in extracts 17 and 18. Pliny's uncle set out from Misenum to rescue friends at Stabiae, where he met his death. Pompeii and Herculaneum were buried in the eruption, and the excavation of these places in modern times supplies us with much information about Roman life in the 1st century A.D.

43. **frigidam:** supply '*aquam*'.

47. **stomacho:** here 'windpipe'.

48. **frequenter interaestuans:** 'subject to chronic inflammation'.

52. **habitus:** 'posture'.

XVIII

1. **adductum:** a participle.

2. **cupere:** this is the infinitive depending on **ais**. Take the order as follows: *Ais te cupere cognoscere.*

3. **ingressus abruperam:** 'Having started to mention it, I had broken off'. He had raised the subject in the previous letter.

5. '**Quamquam animus meminisse horret,**

6. **Incipiam':** Aeneas addresses these words to Dido in Vergil's *Aeneid II* when about to narrate to her the story of the fall of Troy.

8. **mox balineum . . . :** Supply a verb, viz. 'I took'.

10. **tremor terrae:** we know from inscriptions at Pompeii announcing the rebuilding of monuments there that the town had a serious earthquake in A.D. 63.

14. **excitaturus:** 'about to awake her'. **in area domus:** this would be the open space between the house and the sea.

18. **Titi Livii:** the famous historian, see index of proper names.

22. **securitatem:** here 'indifference'.

22. **Nihilo segnius . . . :** supply the verb *sum*.

28. **excedere . . . :** Supply '*excedere oppido nobis est visum*'.

31. **egressi tecta:** Pliny had to get clear of the buildings as there was danger of being trapped under ruined houses.

51. **Miseni quod procurrit abstulerat:** 'it had blotted out the promontory of Misenum'.

52. **orare, hortari, iubere:** historic infinitives giving an impression of anxiety or excitement, 'began to beg . . .'.

56. **(eam) addere gradum cogo:** 'I compelled her to hasten her step.'

62. **et nox:** 'when night came upon us'.

70. **novissimam noctem mundo:** i.e. the end of the world.

72. **illud . . . illud:** different places pointed out by the narrator.

81. **misero:** this should be taken with **solacio.**

85. **cum deficit:** 'when it goes into eclipse'.

89. **suspensam dubiamque noctem spe ac metu exegimus:** 'we spent an anxious night poised between hope and fear'.

91. **lymphati:** 'inspired', almost 'enthusiastic'—to dwell upon the horror of that experience.

94. **donec . . . nuntius:** supply a verb, such as *veniret*.

96. **Haec . . . videbuntur:** Pliny modestly disclaims that the subject-matter is worthy of a letter.

XIX

2. **velim:** the present subjunctive used in polite expressions of this kind: 'I should like'.

   esse: sc. *phantasmata*.

7. **tenuis adhuc et obscurus obtinenti Africam comes haeserat:** 'while still a man of little importance and scarcely known had attached himself as a companion to the man who gained (by lot) the governorship of Africa'. Ex-consuls decided upon acquiring the governorships of Africa and Asia by ballot. Africa and Asia were the two most highly-prized senatorial provinces.

8. **inclinato die:** i.e. during the afternoon siesta.

10. **humana grandior:** Apparations often appeared larger than life to the Romans.

   perterrito Africam se futurorum praenuntiam dixit: 'She said to the frightened man that she was Africa, foreteller of future events'.

17. **futura praeteritis . . . auguratus:** take the order *auguratus futura praeteritis adversa secundis. Praeteritis* and *secundis* are ablatives.

20. **pestilens:** 'unhealthy'.

32. **proscribebatur:** 'a poster was put up'.

38. **sterni sibi:** 'a couch to be made ready for him'. In other contexts this may indicate the making up of a bed, but in this instance the philosopher intended to stay up working.

43. **concuti . . . moveri . . . tollere,** etc.: historic infinitives.

45. **auribusque praetendere:** it is easiest to supply *animum* again: 'he made his mind a protection for his ears'. In other words, he concentrated so hard on his writing that he had no thought of listening for eerie noises.

61. **Domus postea rite conditis manibus caruit:** 'The house afterwards lacked the spirit that had been duly laid'.

68. **Exiguum tempus medium:** 'A short time elapsed'.

74. **nisi forte quod non fui reus:** 'unless perhaps that I was not prosecuted', lit. '. . . not a defendant'.

75. **futurus:** 'but I would have been'.

77. **Caro:** In the reign of Domitian informers were rife and Carus was one of the most notorious. He had been instrumental in securing the death of Pliny's friends. Tacitus mentions him (*Agricola* 45.).

78–80. **quia reis moris est . . . periculi signum fuisse:** This is a rather difficult passage. **submittere capillum** means 'to grow the hair long', a habit of those awaiting trial to draw sympathy to themselves. Translate '. . . because it is a custom of men when accused to let their hair grow long, the cutting of my servant's hair was a sign of the danger thrust aside (*depulsi*)'.

84. **ex altera:** sc. *disputa*.

XX

3. **quamquam via interiacente:** *quamquam* is used with participles sometimes in Pliny. In Augustan prose there would be a finite verb, viz. *interiacet*.

4. **Gerusian:** the Greek word γέρων means an old man. The *Gerousia* was roughly equivalent to an old men's home or almshouse for those who had done good service to the state. **Iseon:** Temples of Isis, the Egyptian goddess, were found in Italy from the first century A.D. There is one at Pompeii, and this eastern cult was well known at Rome.

6. **otiosos et immobiles:** Apparently the crowds were too lazy to attempt to extinguish the flames.

8. **sipho:** another Greek word σίφων, meaning a straw used to suck up liquids. The transition through 'siphon' to 'fire engine' is easy to understand.

11. **collegium:** Originally the *collegia* were voluntary organisations, often formed for some religious purpose, but Julius Caesar and some of the earlier emperors, including Augustus, were obliged to suppress them or take measures against them when they began to resemble trade unions. Often they caused political turmoil and general unrest.

12. **dumtaxat hominum CL:** 'of not more than 150 men'. **ne quis nisi faber recipiatur:** only true workmen were to be admitted.

13. **in aliud utatur:** Pliny means that these men are to be used exclusively as firemen, implying that they will not be allowed to use their position to create disturbances.

XXI

1. **complurium:** sc. *urbium*.

3. **meminerimus:** What tense is this? What kind of a verb is *memini*?

5. **factionibus:** 'associations' here.

7. **hetaeriae:** normally 'brotherhoods', but in this context 'political groups'. **satius est:** 'it would be better'.

10. **ad hoc:** sc. *ad coercendos ignes.*

XXII

1. **domine:** quite a usual form of address used by Pliny to Trajan. Pliny has been accused of abject subservience towards Trajan, but the accusation is, perhaps, exaggerated. **natalem:** sc. *diem.*

3. **fortis aliis super alia operibus:** 'valiant in one good work after another'.

XXIII

1. **Solemne est mihi:** 'It is my rule'. Here *solemne* is to be taken as a noun.

4. **cognitionibus:** more an enquiry conducted by a magistrate than a fixed trial with accusers. The Roman magistrate at these *cognitiones* did however have the right to pass the death sentence (see later in this letter line 16 *duci*).

7. **discrimen aetatum:** i.e. greater leniency for the young —the **teneri.**

10. **nomen ipsum:** translation is made easier if *an* is understood before *nomen.* **flagitia cohaerentia nomini puniantur:** Christianity was regarded in the light of an illegal association, but there was also a belief that the Christians practised cannibalism, probably because the rites of Holy Communion were imperfectly understood.

16. **duci:** to be led out to execution.

17. **pertinaciam . . . obstinationem . . . amentiae:** here is ample proof of the official Roman attitude to the early Christians in the first century A.D. The firmest Christians would obviously have been persecuted most.

21. **ipso tractatu . . . diffundente se crimine:** 'by the very handling as (the number of) charges grew'.

25. **praeeunte me:** 'as I dictated the words'.

27-29. **maledicerent Christo, quorum nihil posse cogi dicuntur qui sunt re vera Christiani:** Here is an unintentional testimonial to the steadfastness of belief that the early Christians possessed.

33. **imaginem tuam:** see also *imagini tuae* above. It was not unusual abroad to require Christians to worship before the statue of a Roman emperor, but this practice was not followed in Rome itself.

38. **carmenque . . . dicere secum invicem:** chanting as in the psalms, when one side of the choir, for instance, *decani*, sings the first part of a verse, and the other side, *cantoris*, responds with the second part. This is known as antiphonal singing.

39. **scelus . . . furta . . . latrocinia . . . adulteria . . . :** these are well-known tenets of the Christian belief, and some of the ten commandments.

41. **ne depositum appellati abnegarent:** 'not to renounce a commitment when called upon to fulfil it'.

44. **cibum, promiscuum tamen et innoxium:** 'food, ordinary however and quite harmless'. Some believed that Christians committed murder and drank blood.

47. **ministrae:** 'deaconesses'.

48. **per tormenta quaerere:** It was quite a normal habit for slaves to be tortured before they gave evidence. Roman law condoned this practice, but Pliny could not have found this duty pleasant.

49. **superstitionem:** 'foreign cult'.

60. **venire:** from *veneo* not *venio*.

XXIV

1. **Actum . . . secutus es:** 'You have pursued a course of action . . .'.

3. **in universum:** Trajan is unwilling to pass general laws that might apply anywhere in the Roman Empire.

4. **Conquirendi non sunt:** 'They are not to be sought out'.

7. **diis:** sc. *dis, deis.*

8. **in praeteritum:** 'in the past'.

9. **sine auctore vero propositi libelli:** Trajan wisely rules that anonymous accusations (*sine auctore* = without signature) should be treated as of no worth at all.

10. **et pessimi exempli, nec nostri saeculi est:** these are genitives of quality: 'for it creates a dangerous precedent and is not characteristic of our times'.

INDEX OF PROPER NAMES

Āfrica, -ae (*f.*): the country of Africa; the S.W. wind blowing from Africa; the tutular genius presiding over Africa.

Āfrĭcus, -a, -um: African; (used as noun), the southwest wind.

Athēnae, -ārum (*f. plur.*) the city of Athens.

Athēnodōrus, -i (*m.*): a philosopher of the Stoic creed.

Augustus, -ī (*m.*): the Emperor Augustus; the title of a later emperor.

Avītus, -ī (*m.*): see **Octavius Avitus**.

Baetica, -ae (*f.*): the southern province of Spain.

Caesar, -aris (*m.*): a title used for an emperor.

Calestrius, -iī (*m.*): see **Tiro**.

Campānia, -ae (*f.*): the district of Italy south of Latium, west of Samnium and north of Lucania, comprising one of the most fertile plains in Italy.

Capreae, -ārum (*f. plur.*): the island of Capri which lies off the promontory of Minerva at the southern end of the Bay of Naples.

Carthāgō, -inis (*f.*): the city of Carthage, once the most important town on the coast of North Africa and grim rival of Rome, had been virtually destroyed by Rome in 146 B.C. In the time of Pliny, Carthage was unimportant.

Cārus, -ī (*m.*): Metius Carus, a notorious informer in the reign of Domitian.

Christiānus, -ī (*m.*): a follower of Christ.

Christus, -ī (*m.*): Christ.

Clitumnus, -ī (*m.*): a small river in Umbria flowing into the Tinia, a tributary of the Tiber; the river god of that name.

Curtius Rūfus: see **Rufus**.

Diāna, -ae (*f.*): the maiden goddess of hunting.

Domitiānus, -ī (*m.*): The Emperor Domitian, who reigned from A.D. 81–96. The latter part of his rule was notorious for acts of great brutality. He was murdered in A.D. 96.

Gerūsia, -ae (*f.*): a home for old men.

Graecus, -ī (*m.*): a Greek.

Hippōnensis, -e: relating to the city of Hippo Regius on the north coast of Numidia, North Africa.

Hispānia, -ae (*f.*): Spain.

Hispellātēs, -ium (*m. plur.*): the inhabitants of Hispellum, (the modern Spello) a town in Umbria, who looked after the bath and inn at the source of the river Clitumnus.

Iseon, -ī (**Iseum, -ī**) (*n.*): a temple of Isis, one of the principal eastern divinities whose worship had spread widely in the Roman empire by the 1st century A.D.

Latīnus, -a, -um: Latin; relating to Latium, the territory in the neighbourhood of Rome.

Laurentīnus, -a, -um: Laurentine; relating to Pliny's estate at Laurentum, an ancient town in Latium not far from the coast.

Līvius, -iī (*m.*): Titus Livius, the famous Roman historian who wrote the *Annales*, dealing with the story of Rome from its foundation in 753 B.C. to the death of Drusus in 9 B.C. He wrote 142 books in all, of which 35 have survived.

Marcus, -ī (*m.*): one of Pliny's freedmen.

Mediōlānum, -ī (*n.*): A city in Gallia Cisalpina which was taken by the Romans in 222 B.C. It became a *municipium* and a colony. Modern Milan is built on its site.

Minerva, -ae (*f.*): Minerva, goddess of wisdom.

Mīsēnum, -ī (*n.*): a promontory in Campania, situated at the northern end of the Bay of Naples; a harbour town on this promontory, some 18 miles distant from Vesuvius.

Nīcomēdensēs, -ium (*m. plur.*): the inhabitants of Nicomedia.

Nīcomēdīa, -ae (*f.*): the capital city of Bithynia, Asia Minor, which became a Roman colony and a favourite resort for Roman emperors.

Octāvius Avītus, -ī (*m.*): a deputy governor at the town of Hippo.

Plīnius, iī (*m.*): For both Pliny the Elder and Pliny the Younger, see Introduction.

Pompōniānus, -ī (*m.*): belonging to Pomponius, a friend of the Elder Pliny who had a house at Stabiae, some four miles from Pompeii.

Rōma, -ae (*f.*): the city of Rome.

Rōmānus, -a, -um: Roman.

Rūfus, -ī (*m.*): Curtius Rufus, an attendant upon the governor of Africa who later returned to Africa as proconsul and died there.

Secundus, -ī (*m.*): The full name of the Younger Pliny was Caius Plinius Caecilius Secundus. For further details see Introduction.

Stabiae, -ārum (*f. pl.*): Stabiae, a town due south of Pompeii on the eastern shore of the Bay of Naples.

Tacitus, -ī (*m.*): Caius Cornelius Tacitus, the famous historian, was a personal friend of Pliny and a few years older than him. His *Histories* dealt with the events from the reign of Galba to the death of Domitian. His *Annals* started at the death of Augustus, A.D. 14, and covered the 54 years to the death of Nero, A.D. 68. He also wrote a treatise on the German nation and a life of Agricola, his father-in-law. Pliny wrote several letters to him, notably those about the eruption of Vesuvius (XVII and XVIII).

Tīcīnum, -ī (*n.*): a city in Cisalpine Gaul, where the modern Pavia now stands.

Tīrō, -ōnis (*m.*): a friend of Pliny, Calestrius Tiro, who served with him in the army and was his colleague as quaestor and praetor.

Tusculānus, -a, -um: relating to Pliny's estate at Tusculum, about 10 miles from Rome.

Tuscus, -a, -um: Tuscan, Etruscan.

Vesuvius, -iī (*m.*): the volcano Vesuvius, dominating the Bay of Naples, which erupted with disastrous consequences in the year A.D. 79.

VOCABULARY

ā, ab (*prep.* with *abl.*): from, by.

abdō, -ere, -didī, -ditum (*v.t.*): to hide.

abdūcō, -ere, -dūxī, -ductum (*v.t.*): to lead away.

abeō, -īre, -īvī or -iī, -itum (*v.i.*): to go away.

abiciō, -ere, -iēcī, -iectum (*v.t.*): to throw away.

abnegō, -āre, -āvī, -ātum (*v.t.*): to refuse, deny.

abrumpō, -ere, -rūpī, -ruptum (*v.t.*): to break off, rend.

abscēdō, -ere, -cessī, -cessum (*v.i.*): to go away, depart.

abscīdō, -ere, -scidī, -scissum (*v.t.*): to cut off.

abscondō, -ere, -condidī, -conditum (*v.t.*): to hide from sight, conceal.

absentia, -ae (*f.*): absence.

absolvō, -ere, -solvī, -solūtum (*v.t.*): to complete, finish, loosen.

absum, abesse, āfuī (*v.i.*): to be absent, distant.

absūmō, -ere, -sūmpsī, -sūmptum (*v.t.*): to consume, take away.

āc (*conj.*): and, and moreover.

accēdō, -ere, -cessī, -cessum (*v.i.*): to approach, come to, be added.

accendō -ere, -ndī, -sum (*v.t.*): to inflame, set alight.

accidō, -ere, -cidī (*v.i.*): to happen.

accipiō, -ere, -cēpī, -ceptum (*v.t.*): to receive, learn.

accūrātus, -a, -um: prepared with care, exact.

accursus, ūs (*m.*): a running, hastening to, concourse.

ācer, -cris, -cre: keen, vigorous, sharp.

acerbus, -a, -um: bitter, painful.

acquīrō, -ere, -sīvī, -sītum (*v.t.*): to add to, obtain, procure.

actus, -ūs (*m.*): action, course of action.

acūmen, -inis (*n.*): shrewdness, discernment.

ad (*prep.* with *acc.*): to, towards, up to, by, near; for, for the purpose of.

addō, -ere, -didī, -ditum (*v.t.*): to add, give in addition.

addere gradum: to gather pace.

addūcō, -ere, -dūxī, -ductum (*v.t.*): to bring, lead to.

adeō (*adv.*): so, to such a degree.

adfectus, -ūs (*m.*): love, sympathy.

adferō, -ferre, attulī, adlātum (*v.t.*): to bring to, bring in, bring forward.

adficiō, -ere, -fēcī, -fectum (*v.t.*): to affect, influence.

adfingō, -ere, -finxī, -fictum (*v.t.*): to shape together, adapt, add.

adfirmō, -āre, -āvī, -ātum (*v.t.*): to assert positively, affirm.

adhūc (*adv.*): thus far, up to now.

adiaceō, -ēre, -uī (*v.i.*): to lie near, adjoin.

adiciō, -ere, -iēcī, -iectum (*v.t.*): to throw up against, throw to, hurl.

adiuvō, -āre, -iūvī, -iūtum (*v.t.*): to help, assist, support.

adlūdō, -ere, -lūsī, -lūsum (*v.t.* and *i*): to play with, joke.

adluō, -ere, -luī (*v.t.*): to wash against.

admittō, -ere, -mīsī, missum (*v.t.*): to let in, let go, come to, admit.

admoneō, -ēre, -monuī, -monitum (*v.t.*): to admonish, warn.

admoveō, -ēre, -mōvī, -mōtum (*v.t.*): to move to, conduct to.

adnatō, -āre (*v.i.*): to swim toward.

adnotō, -āre, -notāvī, -notātum (*v..t*): to write down, take notes.

adnumerō, -āre, -āvī, -ātum (*v.t.*): to count out, add to.

adquiescō, -ere, -ēvī, -ētum (*v.i.*): to derive consolation, find peace.

adsēnsus, ūs (*m.*): assent, approbation.

adsiduus, -a, -um: hardworking, busy.

adspiciō, -ere, -spexī, -spectum (*v.t.*): to look at, perceive.

adstruo, -ere, -strūxī, -structum (*v.t.*): to build near, build in addition.

adsum, -esse, -fuī (*v.i.*): to be at hand, stand by.

adsurgō, -ere, -surrēxī, -surrēctum (*v.i.*): to rise, stand up.

adulterium, -iī (*n.*): adultery.

adventō, -āre, -āvī, -ātum (*v.i.*): to approach, arrive at.

adventus, -ūs (*m.*): arrival.

adversus, -a, -um: opposite, facing, unfavourable, (as noun) adversity.

advesperascit, -āvit (*v. impers.*): evening approaches.

aeger, -ra, -rum: ill, sick.

aegrē (*adv.*): with difficulty.

aequālis, -e: equal.

aequē (*adv.*): equally.

aequō, -āre, -āvī, -ātum (*v.t.*): to make level, make equal, equate.

aestās, -ātis (*f.*): summer.

aestimō, -āre, -āvī, -ātum (*v.t.*): to weigh, value, estimate.

aestuārium, -iī (*n.*): estuary.

aestus, -ūs (*m.*): tide.

aetās, -ātis (*f.*): age.

aeternus, -a, -um: eternal.

aevum, -ī (*n.*): age.

ager, -grī (*m.*): land, territory.

agitātiō, -ōnis (*f.*): continuous motion, agitation, exercise.

agitātor, -ōris (*m.*): driver, charioteer.

agmen, -inis (*n.*): column.

agnoscō, -ere, -nōvī, -nitum (*v.t.*): to recognize.

agō, -ere, ēgī, āctum (*v.t.*): to do, drive, spend, pass, complete; **agere dē:** to treat of, discuss; **gratias agere:** to express thanks.

agrestis, -e: rustic (as noun): country folk.

aiō (*v. defect*): Other forms are **ais, ait, aiunt** (*v.t.*): to say.

albus, -a, -um: white.

aliās (*adv.*): elsewhere.

alibī (*adv.*): elsewhere.

aliēnus, -a, -um: belonging to another.

aliōquī (*adv.*): otherwise, in other respects.

aliquandō (*adv.*): at some time, at last, once.

aliquantō (*adv.*): somewhat, considerably, rather.

aliquī, -qua, -quod: some.

aliquis, aliquis, aliquid (*indef. pron.*): some one, something.

alius, -a, -ud: other, different; **aliī . . . aliī:** some . . . others.

alter: altera: alterum: one of two, the other of two.

alternus, -a, -um: alternate; **alternīs** (sc. *vicibus*): alternately, by turns.

altus, -a, -um: high, deep; altum (*subst.*): the open sea, the deep; in altum: into the deep.

amāns, -ntis (*adj.*): loving; **amantissimus, -a, -um:** most loving.

ambitus, -ūs (*m.*): unlawful striving for power, bribery, corruption.

ambulō, -āre, -āvī, -ātum (*v.i.*): to walk.

ambūrō, -ere, -ussī, -ustum (*v.t.*): to burn round, scorch.

āmentia, -ae (*f.*): folly, madness.

amiciō, -īre, -īcuī or **ixī, -ictum** (*v.t.*): to throw around, wrap.

amīcus, -ī (*m.*): friend.

amita, -ae (*f.*): paternal aunt.

amittō, -ere, -mīsī, -missum (*v.t.*): to lose.

amnis, -is (*m.*): river.

amō, -āre, -āvī, -ātum (*v.t.*): to like, love.

amoenitās, -ātis (*f.*): pleasantness, delightfulness.

amoenus, -a, -um: pleasant, delightful.

amor, -ōris (*m.*): liking, love, affection.

amplector, -ī, -plexus sum (*v.t.*): to embrace.

amplitūdō, -inis (*f.*): size, bulk.

amplus, -a, -um: wide, spacious, splendid.

amputō, -āre, -āvī, -ātum (*v.t.*): to cut away, cut off.

an (*conj.*): whether, or; **utrum ... an:** whether . . . or.

ancilla, -ae (*f.*): maidservant.

angulus, -ī (*m.*): angle, corner, nook.

angustus, -a, -um: narrow.

anima, -ae (*f.*): breath.

animadvertō, -ere, -tī, -sum (*v.t.*): to perceive, notice.

animal, -ālis (*n.*): animal, creature.

animus, -ī (*m.*): mind, intention, feelings, spirit.

annus, -ī (*m.*): year.

ante (*prep.* with *acc.* and *adv.*): before.

antequam (*conj.*) (or **ante quam**): before.

antīquus, -a, -um: ancient, old, former.

aper, -aprī (*m.*): wild boar.

aperiō, -īre, aperuī, apertum (*v.t.*): to open, disclose.

appāreō, -ēre, -uī, -itum (*v.i.*): to open.

appāret (*impers.*): it is clear, evident.

appellō, -āre, -āvī, -ātum (*v.t.*): to call, call upon, name.

apud (*prep.* with *acc.*): at, with, among, before, in the presence of, at the home of.

aqua, -ae (*f.*): water.

arbor, -oris (*f.*): tree.

ārdeō, -ēre, arsī, arsum (*v.i.*): to burn.

ārea, -ae (*f.*): courtyard.

arēna, -ae (*f.*): sand.

arguō, -ere, -uī, ūtum (*v.t.*): to prove, convict, denounce.

ars, artis (*f.*): art.

artifex, -icis (*m.*): an artist, skilled person.

ascendō, -ere, -dī, -sum (*v.i.*): to mount up, climb.

aspiciō, -ere, -spexī, -spectum (*v.t.*): to look at, perceive.

assurgō: see **adsurgo.**

at (*conj.*): but, yet.

āter, -ra, -rum: jet black.

atque (*conj.*): and.

ātrium, -ī (*n.*): hall or principal room of a Roman house, the atrium.

attendō, -ere, -tendī, -tentum (*v.t.*): to direct the attention, consider.

atterō, -ere, -trīvī, -trītum (*v.t.*): to waste away, wear away, consume.

attollō, -ere, no *perf.* or *supine* (*v.t.*): to lift, raise up.

attonitus, -a, -um: astonished.

auctor, -ōris (*m.*): author, adviser, supporter.

auctōritās, -ātis (*f.*): authority, influence.

audācia, -ae (*f.*): boldness, daring, effrontery.

audiō, -īre, -īvī, -ītum (*v.t.*): to hear.

auferō, auferre, abstulī, ablātum: to bear away, carry off.

augeō, -ēre, auxī, auctum (*v.t.*): to increase.

auguror, -ārī, -ātus sum (*v.t.*): to foretell, conjecture, surmise.

auris, -is (*f.*): ear.

aut (*conj.*): or; **aut . . . aut:** either . . . or.

autem (*conj.*): but, now, moreover.

autumnus, -ī (*m.*): autumn.

auxilium, -iī (*n.*): help.

avidus, -a, -um: greedy, eager, covetous.

āvocō, -āre, -āvī, -ātum (*v.t.*): to call away, divert, distract.

avunculus, -ī (*m.*): a maternal uncle.

avus, -ī (*m.*): grandfather.

balineum, -ī (*n.*): bathroom, bath.

barba, -ae (*f.*): beard.

bene, melius, optimē (*adv.*): well.

bibō, -ere, bibī (*v.t.*): drink.

brevis, -e: short; **brevī:** in a short time, briefly.

C: Caius.

calculus, -ī (*m.*): a small stone, pebble.

calidus, -a, -um: warm, hot.

cālīgō, -inis (*f.*): mist, gloom, darkness.

campus, -ī (*m.*): plain, field.

candidus, -a, -um: bright, white.

canis, -is (*c.*): dog.

cantō, -āre, -āvī, -ātum (*v.t.*): to sing.

capax, -ācis: wide, spacious.

capillus, -ī (*m.*): hair of head or beard.

capiō, -ere, cēpī, captum (*v.t.*): to take.

caput, capitis (*n.*): head.

careō, -ēre, -uī, -itum (*v.i.* with *abl.*): to be without, be deprived of.

cāritās, -ātis (*f.*): love, affection.

carmen, -inis (*n.*): song.

castigō, -āre, -āvī, -ātum (*v.t.*): to reprove, censure, correct an error.

castitās, -ātis (*f.*): purity, chastity.

cāsus, -ūs (*m.*): fate, misfortune.

catēna, -ae (*f.*): chain, fetter.

causa, -ae (*f.*): cause, reason, case; (preceded by *genit.*) on account of, for the sake of.

cautus, -a, -um: cautious, wary.

cavaedium, -iī (*n.*): inner court.

cēdō, cēdere, cessī, cessum (*v.i.*): to yield.

celebrō, -āre, -āvī, -ātum (*v.t.*): to frequent, fill.

cēna, -ae (*f.*): dinner, supper.

cēnō, -āre, -āvī, -ātum (v.i.): to dine.

cēra, -ae (f.): wax.

cernō, -ere, crēvī, crētum (v.t.): to distinguish, perceive, see.

certāmen, -inis (n.): struggle, contest.

certātim (adv.): eagerly.

certē (adv.): certainly, at any rate.

certō, -āre, -āvī, -ātum (v.t.): to contend, vie with.

certus, -a, -um: sure, accurate, certain.

cessō, -āre, -āvī, -ātum (v.i. and t.): to delay, linger.

cēterī, -ae, -a: the rest, all other.

cibus, -ī (m.): food.

cingō, -ere, cīnxī, cīnctum (v.t.): to surround.

cinis, -eris (m. rarely f.): ashes.

circā (adv. and prep.): around.

circēnsis, -e: relating to the circus; circēnsēs -ium (m.plur.) circus, race-course.

circum (prep. with acc.): around, about, near.

circumagō, -ere, -ēgī, -āctum (v.t.): to set in circular motion, turn round, wheel.

circumeō, -īre, -iī, -itum (v.t.): to travel round, inspect.

circumiaceō, -ēre, -uī (v.i.): to lie around, border on.

cithara, -ae (f.): lute, guitar.

cito (adv.): quickly, speedily.

cīvis, cīvis (c.): citizen.

cīvitās, -ātis (f.): community, state.

clāmitō, -āre, -āvī, -ātum (v.i. and t.): to cry aloud frequently.

clāmor, -ōris (m.): shout, call, cry, applause.

clārē (adv.): clearly, distinctly, brightly.

clāritās, -ātis (f.): clearness, brightness.

clārus, -a, -um: clear, bright.

classis, -is (f.): fleet.

claudō, -ere, clausī, clausum (v.t.): to shut.

coeō, -īre, -iī, -itum (v.i. and t.): to meet, come together.

coepī, -pisse (v.i.): began.

coerceō, -ēre, -uī, -itum (v.t.): to control, compel, restrain.

cōgitātiō, -ōnis (f.): thought, meditation.

cōgitō, -āre, -āvī, -ātum (v.t. and i.): to think, consider, reflect.

cognitiō, -ōnis (f.): learning, judicial enquiry.

cognōscō, -ere, -nōvī, -nitum (v.t.): to get to know, find out.

cōgō, -ere, coēgī, coāctum (v.t.): to compel, collect.

cohaereō, -ēre, -sī, -sum (v.i.): to stick, adhere to.

collātiō, -ōnis (f.): contribution, collection.

collēgium, -iī (n.): union, guild.

colligō, -ere, collēgī, collēctum (v.t.): to collect, conclude, deduce.

collis, -is (m.): hill.

collocō, -āre, -āvī, -ātum (v.t.): to place, set up, erect.

collūsor, -ōris (m.): playfellow, companion.

colōnia, -ae (f.): landed estate, farm, colony, colonial town.

colōnus, -ī (m.): farmer, husbandman, tenant.

color, -ōris (m.): colour.

columna, -ae (f.): column, pillar.

comes, -itis (c.): companion, comrade.

comitor, -ārī, -ātus sum (v.t.): to accompany, follow, attend.

commendō, -āre, -āvī, -ātum (*v.t.*): to commit to, commend to.

committō, -ere, -mīsī, -missum (*v.t.*): to entrust, commit.

commoror, -ārī, -ātus sum (*v.i.*): to stop, stay, wait, delay.

communicō, -āre, -āvī, -ātum (*v.t.*): to share, make common.

cōmoedus, -ī (*m.*): comedian, comic actor.

compārō, -āre, -āvī, -ātum: (*v.t.*): to procure.

compēs, -pedis (*f.*): shackle, fetter.

compescō, -ere, -uī (*v.t.*): to confine, restrain, quench.

complūrēs, -ium: several.

compōnō, -ere, -posuī, -positum (*v.t.*): to settle, compose.

concēdō, -ere, -cessī, -cessum (*v.t. and i.*): to concede, yield, allow.

concerpō, -ere, -cerpsī, -cerptum (*v.t.*): to pluck up, tear up.

concido, -ere, -cidī (*v.i.*): to fall down.

concipiō, -ere, -cēpī, -ceptum (*v.t.*): to take up, conceive.

concordia, ae (*f.*): harmony, agreement.

concurrō, -ere, -currī, -cursum (*v.i.*): to run together, assemble, engage in conflict.

concutiō, -ere, -cussī, -cussum (*v.i.*): to shake together, shatter.

condō, -ere, condidī, conditum (*v.t.*): to build, found, lay (of a ghost).

condūcō, -ere, -dūxī, ductum (*v.t.*): to take on lease, hire.

cōnfectus, -a um: exhausted.

cōnferō, -ferre, -tulī, -lātum (*v.t.*) to bring, collect, compare; **se cōnferre:** to go.

cōnficiō, -ere -fēcī, -fectum (*v.t.*) to complete, accomplish.

cōnfīdo, -ere, -fīsus sum (*v.i.* or with *dat.* or *abl.*) to trust, reply on.

cōnfiteor, -ērī, -fessus sum (*v.t.*): to confess, admit.

cōnfluō, -ere, -flūxī (*v.i.*): to flow together.

congruō, -ere, congruī (*v.i.*): to agree, flock together.

coniectō, -āre, -āvī, -ātum (*v.t.*): to conjecture, guess.

coniunx, -iugis (*c.*): wife, spouse, coincide.

conquīrō, -ere, -quīsīvī, -quīsītum (*v.t.*): to search for, seek out.

cōnsentiō, -īre, -sēnsī, -sēnsum (*v.i.*): to agree, assent. to.

cōnsequor, -ī, -secūtus sum (*v.t.*): to attain, achieve, reach.

cōnsīderō, -āre, -āvī, -ātum (*v.t.*): to consider, examine, reflect.

cōnsīdō, -ere, -sēdī, -sessum (*v.i.*): to sit down, settle.

cōnsilium, -iī (*n.*): plan, policy, judgment, advice.

cōnsistō, -ere, -stitī, -stitum (*v.i.*): to stand, keep one's place, halt.

cōnspiciō, -ere, -spexī, -spectum (*v.t.*): to catch sight of, see.

cōnspīrō, -āre, -āvī, -ātum (*v.i.*): to unite, combine, be in harmony.

cōnstantia, -ae (*f.*): steadfastness.

cōnstō, -āre, -stitī (*v.i.*): to be established; **cōnstat** (*impers.*): it is agreed.

cōnstituō, -ere, -uī, -ūtum (*v.t.*): to draw up, fix, settle, resolve.

cōnsuēscō, -ere, -suēvī, -suētum (*v.i.*): to grow accustomed, be wont.

cōnsuētūdō, -inis (f.): habit, custom, way of life.

cōnsul, -ulis (m.): consul.

cōnsulō, -ere, -suluī, -sultum (v.t. and i.): to consult, ask advice°of; (with dat.): to act in the interests of.

cōnsultātiō, -ōnis (f.): consultation, deliberation.

contāgiō, -ōnis (f.): touching, contagion.

contemnō, -ere, -tempsī, -temptum (v.t.): to scorn, despise.

conterō, -ere, -trīvī, -trītum (v.t.): to wear out, waste.

continentia, -ae (f.): abstemiousness, temperance, moderation.

contineō, -ēre, -uī, -tentum (v.t. and i.): to connect, comprise, involve, hold in check, limit, restrain.

contrā (adv. and prep. with acc.): on the other hand, against.

contrahō, -ere, -trāxī, -tractum (v.t.): to draw together, bring together.

contrārius, -a, -um: contrary, conflicting.

contubernium, -iī (n.): dwelling together in a tent, companionship.

contumēlia, -ae (f.): insult, affront.

contus, -ī (m.): pole.

convalescō, -ere -uī (v.i.): to regain health, grow strong.

conveniō, -īre, -vēnī, -ventum (v.i.): to come together.

convenit (impers.): it is fitting, it is becoming.

convictor, -ōris (m.): fellow-diner, messmate.

cōpia, -ae (f.): supply, abundance; (plur.) forces.

corpus, -ōris (n.): body.

corrigō, -ere, -rēxī, -rēctum (v.t.): to straighten, amend, correct.

corripiō, -ere, -ripuī, -reptum (v.t.): to seize upon, snatch.

corrumpō, -ere, -rūpī, -ruptum (v.t.): to break through, corrupt.

cotīdiē (adv.): daily, every day.

crassus, -a, -um: solid, thick, dense.

crēbrescō, -ere, crēbruī (v.i.): to become frequent, grow strong.

crēdō, -ere, crēdidī, crēditum (v.i.): to believe.

crescō, -ere, crēvī, crētum (v.i.): to grow.

crīmen, -inis (n.): charge, accusation, trial, crime.

crūs, crūris (n.): leg.

cryptoporticus, -ūs (m.): covered portico.

cubiculum, -ī (n.): bedroom, sitting room.

cubō, -āre, cubuī, cubitum (v.i.): to lie down, recline.

culpa, -ae (f.): blame, fault.

culter, -trī (m.): knife.

cum (prep. with abl.): with; (conj.): since, when.

cunctātiō, -ōnis (f.): tarrying, delay.

cunctor, -ārī, -ātus sum (v.i.): to tarry, delay.

cunctus, -a, -um: all, entire.

cupiō, -ere, cupīvī, cupītum (v.t.): to desire, long for.

cupressus, -ī (f.): cypress.

cūra, -ae (f.): care, anxiety.

cūrō, -āre, -āvī, -ātum (v.t.) (with acc. and gerund): to care for, cause to be done.

currō, -ere, cucurrī, cursum (v.i.): to run.

currus, -ūs (*m.*): carriage, chariot.

cursus, -ūs (*m.*): course, way.

custodiō, -īre, -īvī, -ītum (*v.t.*): to guard, pretect, defend.

D: the letter D, 500.

damnō, -āre, āvī, ātum (*v.t.*): to condemn.

dē (*prep.* with *abl.*): from, down from, about, concerning.

debeō, -ēre, -uī, -itum (*v.t.*): to owe, ought, must.

dēcēdō, -ere, -cessī, -cessum (*v.i.*): to go away, depart.

decet, decēre, decuit (*impers.* with *acc.*): it is fitting, suitable, proper.

dēcurro, -ere, -cucurrī or **-currī, -cursum** (*v.t.* and *i.*): to run down, hurry, have recourse to.

dēdō, -ere, dēdidī, dēditum (*v.t.*): to give up, surrender.

dēferō, -ferre, -tulī, -lātum (*v.t.*): to carry down, report.

dēficiō, -ere, -fēcī, -fectum (*v.i.*): to fail, eclipse, revolt.

deflectō, -ere, -flexī, -flexum (*v.i.* and *t.*): to turn aside.

defleō, -ēre, -flēvī, -flētum (*v.t.*): to weep over, deplore, bewail.

dēfungor, -ī, -functus sum (*v.i.*) (with *abl.*): to discharge, perform, die.

dēfunctus, -ī (*m.*): a dead man.

dehiscō, -ere, -hīvī (*v.i.*): to gape open, yawn.

dein, deinde (*adv.*): secondly, next, then.

dēlectō, -āre, -āvī, -ātum (*v.t.*): to delight, please, charm.

delphīnus, -ī (*m.*): dolphin.

dēprehendō, -ere, -dī, -sum (*v.t.*): to catch, detect.

dēmum (*adv.*): at last, at length.

dēnique (*adv.*): at length, finally, to sum up.

dēnsus, -a, -um: thick.

dēpellō, -ēre, -pulī, -pulsum (*v.t.*): to drive out, remove, dislodge.

dēpōnō, -ere, -posuī, -positum (*v.t.*): to lay aside, abandon, put down.

dēpositum, -ī (*n.*): deposit.

dēscendō, -ere, -dī, -sum (*v.i.*): to climb down, descend.

dēserō, -ere, -seruī, -sertum (*v.t.*): to leave, desert.

dēsideō, -ere, -sēdī (*v.i.*): to sit down, remain idle.

dēsīderium, -iī (*n.*): yearning, longing.

dēsīderō, -āre, -āvī, -ātum (*v.t.*): to miss, long for, want.

dēsinō, -ere, -sīvī, -situm (*v.t.* and *i.*): to cease, stop.

dēspērō, -āre, -āvī, -ātum (*v.t.* and *i.*): to despair of, give up.

dēstituō, -ere, -uī, -ūtum (*v.t.*): to set down, forsake, abandon.

dēsum, -esse, -fuī (*v.i.*): to be wanting; (with *dat.*) fail, neglect.

detineō, -ēre, -tinuī, -tentum (*v.t.*): to hold back, keep back.

dētondeō, -ēre, -totondī and **-tondī, -tōnsum** (*v.t.*): to shear off, cut off.

dēvexitās, -ātis (*f.*): a sloping.

dexter, -tra, -trum (and **-tera, -terum**): right, on the right.

deus, -ī (*m.*): god.

diaeta, -ae (*f.*): dining room, summer house.

dīcō, -ere, dīxī, dictum (*v.t.*): to say, speak.

dictitō, -āre, -āvī, -ātum (*v.t.*): to say often, assert repeatedly.

dictō, -āre, -āvī, -ātum (*v.t.*): to say repeatedly, dictate for writing.

diēs, -ēī (*m.*): day; **in diēs**: from day to day; **in diem**: for the present hour.

differō, -ferre, distulī, dīlātum (*v.t.*): to postpone, adjourn; (*v.i.*): to differ.

difficilis, -e: difficult.

diffundō, -ere, -fūdī, -fūsum (*v.t.*): to spread out, scatter, extend.

digitus, -ī (*m.*): finger.

dignus, -a, -um: worthy, suitable, worthy of.

dīgredior, ī, -gressus sum (*v.i.*): to go away, depart.

dīlabor, ī, -lāpsus sum (*v.i.*): to glide away, disappear.

dīligēns, -ntis: careful, diligent.

dīligō, -ere, -lēxī, -lēctum (*v.t.*): to love.

dīmētior, -īrī, mēnsus sum (*v.t.*): to measure out.

dīmittō, -ere, -mīsī, -missum (*v.t.*): to send away, dismiss.

dīrus, -a, -um: fearful, awful.

discēdō, -ere, -cessī, -cessum (*v.i.*): to withdraw, depart.

discernō, -ere, -crēvī, -crētum (*v.t.*): to separate, part, divide.

discō, -ere, didicī (*v.t.*): to learn.

discrībō (dēscrībō), -ere, -scrīpsī, -scriptum (*v.t.*): to divide, apportion.

discrīmen, -inis (*n.*): separation, crisis, distinction.

discursus, -ūs (*m.*): running about, a rushing.

dispiciō, -ere, -spexī, -spectum (*v.i. & t.*): to gaze, consider, reflect.

dispōnō, -ere, -posuī, -positum (*v.t.*): to arrange, place at intervals, post.

disputō, -āre, -āvi, -ātum (*v.t.*): to estimate, discuss.

distinguō, -ere, -nxī, -nctum (*v.t.*): to mark off, separate.

diū (*adv.*): for a long time.

dīvus (dīus) -a, um: divine (used as *noun*): god.

dīversus, -a, -um: different, contrary, separate.

dīvidō, -ere, -vīsī, -vīsum (*v.t.*): to divide, separate.

dō, dare, dedī, datum (*v.t.*): to give; **dare operam**: to take pains.

doceō, -ēre, -uī, doctum (*v.t.*): to teach, explain.

dominus, -ī (*m.*): master, lord; also used as title for emperor.

domus, -ūs (*f.*): house, home; **domī**: at home.

dōnec (*adv.*): until, as long as.

dormiō, -īre, -īvī, -ītum (*v.i.*): to sleep.

dubitō, -āre, -āvī, -ātum (*v.t.*): to doubt, hesitate.

dubius, -a, -um: doubtful, uncertain.

dūcō, -ere, dūxī, ductum (*v.t.*): to lead, consider.

dulcēdō, -inis (*f.*): sweetness, charm.

dumtaxat (*adv.*): to this extent, so far, exactly.

duo, duae, duo: two.

duodēvīcēnsimus, -a, -um: eighteenth.

dūrō, -āre, -āvī, -ātum (*v.t. and i.*): to make hard, harden.

dūrus, -a, -um: hard, harsh.

ē, ex (*prep.* with *abl.*): out of, from.

ecce: see, behold.

ecquis, ecquid (*interr. pron.*): is there anyone, anything? whether.

ēdictum, I (*n.*): proclamation, edict.

ēdiscō, -ere, -didicī (*v.t.*): to learn thoroughly, learn by heart.

ēdūcō, -āre, -āvī, -ātum (*v.t.*): to bring up, rear, educate.

ēdūcō, -ere, -dūxī, -ductum (*v.t.*): to lead out.

efferō, -ferre, extulī, ēlātum (*v.t.*): to bring forth, carry out, remove, raise, extol.

effigiēs, -ēī (*f.*): ghost.

effodiō, -ere, -fōdī, -fossum (*v.t.*): to dig out, dig up.

effulgeō, -ēre, effulsī (*v.i.*): to shine, gleam, glitter.

effundō, -ere, -fūdī, -fūsum (*v.t.*): to pour forth, shed.

ego: I.

ēgredior, -ī, -gressus sum (*v.t. and v.i.*): to go out, disembark.

ēgregius, -a, -um: splendid, excellent, distinguished.

ēligō, -ere, -lēgī, -lectum (*v.t.*): to choose, select.

ēluctor, -ārī, -ātus sum (*v.t. and i.*): to force a way through.

ēmendātiō, -ōnis (*f.*): correction, emendation.

ēmendō, -āre, -āvī, -ātum (*v.t.*): to correct, amend.

ēmergō, -ere, -mersī, -mersum (*v.i.*): to emerge, raise, come forth.

emō, -ere, -ēmī, emptum (*v.t.*): to buy.

emptor, -ōris (*m.*): buyer.

enim (*conj.*): for.

ēnotō, -āre, -āvī, -ātum (*v.t.*): to note down.

eō (*adv.*): to that place, thither; **eō magis:** all the more.

eō, īre, īvī, itum (*v.i.*): to go.

epistula, -ae (*f.*): letter.

equus, -ī (*m.*): horse.

ergō (*adv.*): therefore.

ēripiō, -ere, -ripuī, -reptum (*v.t.*): to snatch away.

error, -ōris (*m.*): error, mistake.

ērudītiō, -ōnis (*f.*): instruction, learning.

ērudītus, -a, -um: learned, accomplished.

et (*conj.*): and; **et . . . et . . . :** both . . . and. . . .

etiam (*conj.*): also, and, even.

etiamsī and **etiam sī** (*conj.*): even if.

ēvādō, -ere, -vādī, -vāsum (*v.i.*): to fall out, turn out, get away, escape.

ēvānescō, -ere, -vānuī (*v.i.*): to vanish, pass away.

ēvehō, -ere, -vēxī, -vectum (*v.t.*): to carry forth.

ēventus, -ūs (*m.*): result, fortune.

ēvertō, -ere, -vertī, -versum (*v.t.*): to overthrow, destroy.

ēvigilō, -āre, -āvī, -ātum (*v.t. and i.*): to wake up, awake.

exaequō, -āre, -āvī, -ātum (*v.t. and i.*): to make equal or level.

excēdō, -ere, -cessī, -cessum (*v.i. and t.*): to go out.

excerpo, -ere, -psī, -ptum (*v.t.*): to pick out, make selections.

excidō, -ere, -cidī (*v.i.*): to fall out or down, slip out, escape.

excipiō, -ere, -cēpī, -ceptum (*v.t.*): to catch, receive eagerly, sustain.

excitō, -āre, -āvī, -ātum (*v.t.*): to arouse, stimulate, excite, incite.

exclūdō, -ere, -clūsī, -clūsum (*v.t.*): to shut out, exclude, hinder.

excurrō, -ere, -cucurrī or **currī, -cursum** (*v.t. and i.*): to run out, sally forth.

excutiō, -ere, -cussī, -cussum (*v.t.*): to sift, examine, shake off, cast out.

exedō, -esse, -ēdī, -ēsum (*v.t.*): to eat up, consume, devour.

exemplum, -ī (*n.*): example, pattern.

exeō, -īre, -iī, -itum (*v.i.*): to go out, go away, depart.

exerceō, -ēre, -uī, -itum (*v.t.*): to work thoroughly, drill, exercise.

exigō, -ere, -ēgī, -āctum (*v.t.*): to spend, pass, to drive out, thrust out.

exiguus, -a, -um: scanty, small.

ex(s)iliō, -īre, -uī (*v.i.*): to leap out, spring forth.

exīmō, -ere, -ēmī, -emptum (*v.t.*): to take away, remove.

expediō, -īre, -īvī, -ītum (*v.t.*): to free, extricate.

experimentum, -ī (*n.*): trial, experiment.

experior, -īrī, -pertus sum (*v.t.*): to try, experience, put to the test.

expōnō, -ere, -posuī, -positum (*v.t.*): to send forth, explain, expound.

exprimō, -ere, -pressī, -pressum (*v.t.*): to portray, express, press.

exsiliō (exiliō), -ire, -siluī (*v.i.*): to spring up, leap forth.

ex(s)pectō, -āre, -āvī, -ātum (*v.t.*): to look out for, await.

ex(s)tinguō, -ere, -nxī, -nctum (*v.t.*): to extinguish, quench.

extendō, -ere, -dī, -sum and **tum** (*v.t.*): to extend, protract.

extrahō, -ere, -trāxī, -tractum (*v.t.*): to draw out, extract.

faber, -rī (*m.*): smith, artisan, fireman.

facile (*adv.*): easily.

faciō, -ere, fēcī, factum (*v.t.*): to do, make.

factiō, -ōnis (*f.*): side, faction.

facultās, -ātis (*f.*): chance, opportunity, ability.

falsō (*adv.*): falsely.

fāma, -ae (*f.*): report, rumour, fame, glory.

familiāris, -e: relating to slaves or servants.

familiāris, -is (*m.*): a familiar acquaintance, friend.

familiāriter (*adv.*): familiarly, intimately.

fateor, -ērī, fassus sum (*v.t.* and *i.*): to admit, confess.

fātidicus, -a, -um: prophetic, prophesying.

faveō, -ēre, fāvī, fautum (*v.i.*) (with *dat.*): to favour, be well-disposed to, befriend.

favor, -ōris (*m.*): favour, support.

fax, facis (*f.*): torch, firebrand.

fēlix, -icis: happy.

fēmina, -ae (*f.*): woman.

fenestra, -ae (*f.*): window.

ferē (*adv.*): almost, nearly, about.

ferō, ferre, tulī, lātum (*v.t.*): to bear, carry, produce.

ferrum, -ī (*n.*): iron.

festīnātiō, ōnis (*f.*): haste, speed.

festīvus, -a, -um: lively, gay, festive.

fidēs, -ēī (*f.*): faith, loyalty, trustworthiness.

fīdūcia, -ae (*f.*): confidence, trust.

figūra, -ae (*f.*): shape, appearance, form.

fīlia, -ae (*f.*): daughter.

fīlius, -ī (*m.*): son.

fingō, -ere, finxī, fictum (*v.t.*): to invent, imagine, shape, form.

finiō, -īre, -īvī or **-iī, -ītum** (*v.t.*): to finish.

finis, -is (*m.*): boundary, limit, end.

finitimus, -a, -um: neighbouring, adjoining.

fiō, -fierī, factus sum (*v.i.*): to happen, become, be done.

firmō, -āre, -āvi, -ātum (*v.t.*): to strengthen, fortify, secure.

flāgitium, -iī (*n.*): crime, disgraceful act, sin.

flamma, -ae (*f.*): flame, blaze.

flectō, -ere, -xī, -xum (*v.t.*): to bend, turn, direct.

flōreō, -ēre, -uī (*v.i.*): to flourish, bloom, be eminent.

fluctus, -ūs (*m.*): wave.

fluitō, -āre, -āvī, -ātum (*v.i.*): to float.

flūmen, -inis (*n.*): river.

folium, -iī (*n.*): leaf.

fōmentum, -ī (*n.*): lotion, poultice, comfort.

fōns, fontis (*m.*): fountain, source.

fore: *fut. infin.* of **sum:** See **sum.**

forma, -ae (*f.*): shape.

formīdō, -inis (*f.*): fear, terror.

formīdulōsus, -a, -um: fearful, terrible.

formō, -āre, -āvī, -ātum (*v.t.*): to form, fashion, set, compose.

fortasse (*adv.*): perhaps, possibly.

forte (*abl.* of **fors** used as *adv.*): by chance.

fortis, e: strong, brave.

fortūna, -ae (*f.*): fortune, fate.

forum, -ī (*n.*): market place, forum.

fragor, -ōris (*m.*): noise, crash.

frangō, -ere, frēgī, frāctum (*v.t.*): to break.

frāter, -tris (*m.*): brother.

fraxinus, -ī (*f.*): ash-tree.

frequēns, -ntis: frequent.

frequenter (*adv.*): often, frequently.

frequentō, -āre, -āvī, -ātum (*v.t.*): to visit or resort to frequently.

frīgidus, -a, -um: cold, tame; **frīgida (aqua):** cold water; (XVII, 4) a cold bath.

frōns, frontis (*f.*): forehead, front.

frūgālitās, -ātis (*f.*): temperance, thriftiness.

frūgi (*dat.* of **frux**): useful, fit, proper.

fruor, fruī, frūctus sum (or **fruitus sum**) (*v.i.*): to enjoy.

fuga, -ae (*f.*): flight, rout, escape.

fugiō, -ere, fūgī, fugitum (*v.t.* and *i.*): to avoid, flee.

fulciō, -īre, fulsī, fultum (*v.t.*): to prop up, stay, support.

fulgor, -ōris (*m.*): brightness, lightning.

fūmus, -ī (*m.*): smoke, steam.

furtum, -ī (*n.*): theft, robbery.

gaudeō, -ēre, gāvisus sum (*v.i.* semi-dep.): to rejoice.

gaudium, -iī (*n.*): joy.

gemitus, -ūs (*m.*): groan, complaint.

genus, -eris (*n.*): kind, class, family, type.

gerō, -ere, gessī, gestum (*v.t.*): to carry, carry on, wage, hold (office), transact.

gestātor, -ōris (*m.*): bearer, carrier.

gestō, -āre, -āvī, -ātum (*v.t.*): to bear, carry.

glōria, -ae (*f.*): glory, renown, fame.

glōrior, -ārī, -ātus sum (*v.i.*): to boast, glory in.

gradātim (*adv.*): by degrees.

gradus, -ūs (*m.*): step.

grandis, -e: full-grown, large, great.

grātia, -ae (*f.*): favour, esteem.
grātiās agere: to give thanks.

grātus, -a, -um: pleasing.

gravis, -e: heavy, ponderous.

gravitās, -ātis (*f.*): weight, severity, vehemence.

gremium, -iī (*n.*): lap, bosom, centre.

gubernāculum, -ī (*n.*): helm, rudder.

gubernātor, -ōris (*m.*): helmsman, pilot.

gula, -ae (*f.*): gullet, gluttony.

gurges, -itis (*m.*): whirlpool, stream.

gustō, -āre, -āvī, -ātum (*v.t.*): to taste.

gymnasium, -iī (*n.*): gymnasium.

habeō, -ēre, -uī, -itum (*v.t.*): to have, hold, possess, consider.

habitātiō, -ōnis (*f.*): lodging, dwelling, place.

habitus, ūs (*m.*): appearance, posture.

haereō, -ēre, haesī, haesum (*v.i.*): to stick join, attach oneself to.

haesitō, -āre, -āvī, -ātum (*v.i.*): to stick fast, hesitate, be at a loss.

hama, -ae (*f.*): a water bucket, fire bucket.

harēna, -ae (*f.*): sand.

hauriō, -īre, hausī, haustum (*v.t.*): to drink, drain.

herba, -ae (*f.*): grass.

hercule: by Hercules!

hetaeria, -ae (*f.*): a religious brotherhood, fraternity.

heus!: I say!, look now!

hībernāculum, -ī (*n.*): a winter apartment, winter residence.

hic, haec, hoc: this.

hīc (*adv.*): here.

hiems (hiemps), hiemis (*f.*): winter, storm, bad weather.

hilaris, -e: gay, blithe.

hinc (*adv.*): from this place, hence.

historia, -ae (*f.*): history, narrative.

homō, -inis (*m.*): man.

honestus, -a, -um: honourable, respectable, worthy.

honōs (honor), -ōris (*m.*): honour, office, esteem.

hōra, -ae (*f.*): hour.

horrendus, -a, -um: dreadful, horrible.

horrēns, -ntis: bristling.

horreō, -ere, -uī (*v.i.* and *t.*): to stand on end, bristle, tremble.

hortor, -ārī, -ātus sum (*v.t.*): to urge, exhort.

hospitium, -iī (*n.*): hostel, inn.

hūc (*adv.*): hither, to this, in this direction.

hūmānitās, -ātis (*f.*): culture, good nature.

hūmānus, -a, -um: human, humane.

iaceō, -ēre, iacuī (*v.i.*): to lie, lie down.

iaciō, -ere, iēcī, iactum (*v.t.*): to throw.

iam (*adv.*): now, already.

ibi (*adv.*): there.

īdem, eadem, idem: same.

identidem (*adv.*): repeatedly, several times.

ideō (*adv.*): for that reason, on that account.

īdōlon, -ī (*n.*): spectre, apparition.

igitur (*conj.*): therefore.

ignārus, -a, um: ignorant of.

igneus, -a, -um: fiery.

ignis, -is (*m.*): fire.

ignorantia, -ae (*f.*): ignorance.

illāc (*adv.*): by that side, in that direction.

illaesus, -a, -um: unhurt, unharmed.

ille, -a, -ud: that, that well-known person, he, she, it.

illīterātus, -a, -um: unlettered, uncultured.

illūc (*adv.*): thither.

illucēscō, -ere, -lūxī (*v.i.*): to grow light, dawn.

illūnis, -e: moonless, without moonlight.

imāgo, -inis (*f.*): likeness, image, statue.

immātūrus, -a, -um: untimely, immature.

immineō, -ēre (*v.i.*): to overhang, impend.

immō (*adv.*): nay rather, on the contrary.

immōbilis, -e: motionless.

immodicus, -a, -um: excessive, unreasonable.

immortālis, -e: immortal, eternal.

impar, imparis: unequal.

impellō, -ere, -pulī, -pulsum (*v.t.*): to drive, impel.

impendō, -ere, -dī, -sum: (*v.t.*): to spend upon, expend.

imperium, -iī (*n.*): command, imperial authority.

impetrō, -āre, -āvī, -ātum (*v.t.*): to obtain, gain a request.

implicitus, -a, -um: involved, attached.

implicō, -āre, -āvī, -ātum (*v.t.*): to enwrap, embrace.

impōnō, -ere, -posuī, -positum (*v.t.*): to place, lay upon, impose upon.

imprudentia, -ae (*f.*): want of foresight, imprudence, ignorance.

imputō, -āre, -āvī, -ātum (*v.t.*): to reckon, impute, ascribe.

in (*prep.* with *acc.*): to, towards, into, against; (with *abl.*): in, on, among.

inānis, -e: empty, idle.

incalescō, -ere, -caluī (*v.i.*): to grow warm.

incendium, -iī (*n.*): fire.

incertus, -a, -um: uncertain, vague.

inchoō, -āre, -āvī, -ātum (*v.t.*): to begin.

incidō, -ere, -cidī, -cāsum (*v.i.*): to fall, fall upon, happen, come to light.

incipiō, -ere, -cēpī, -ceptum (*v.t.*): to begin.

incitāmentum, -ī (*n.*): incitement, inducement.

inclīno, -are, -āvī, -ātum (*v.t.* and *i.*): to bend down, sink.

inclūdō, -ere, -clūsī, -clūsum (*v.t.*): to shut in, confine.

incolumis, -e: safe, sound.

incrēdibilis, -e: unbelievable, incredible, extraordinary.

incumbō, -ere, cubuī, -cubitum (*v.i.*): to lean or recline upon.

incūsō, -āre, -āvī, -ātum (*v.t.*): to accuse, find fault with.

inde (*adv.*): thence, then.

index, -icis (*c.*): a forefinger, informer.

indicium, -iī (*n.*): sign, proof, mark.

indicō, -āre, -āvī, -ātum (*v.t.*): to point out, declare, disclose.

indignus, -a, -um: unworthy.

indolēs, -is (*f.*): genius, talent.

indūcō, -ere, -dūxī, -ductum (v.t.): to lead on, induce.

induō, -ere, -uī, -utum (v.t.): to put on, dress.

inerrō, -āre, -āvī, -ātum (v.i.): to wander about, flit.

inertia, -ae (f.): idleness, laziness.

īnfāmis, -e: of ill repute, notorious.

īnfāns, -ntis (as subst.): child, infant.

īnfantia, -ae (f.): infancy, childhood.

īnferō, -ferre, intulī, illātum (v.t.): to bring in, bear into.

īnfrā (adv.): below.

īnfūsus, a, -um: poured over.

ingenium, -iī (n.): nature, character, natural ability.

ingēns, -ntis: huge, vast, enormous.

ingredior, -ī, -gressus sum (v.t.): to enter.

ingressus, -ūs (m.): entry, beginning.

inhabitō, -āre, -āvī, -ātum (v.t.): to dwell in, inhabit.

inhibeō, -ēre, -uī, -itum (v.t.): to curb, check, restrain.

initium, -iī (n.): beginning; initiō: at the beginning, at first.

innitor, -ī, -nixus sum (nīsus sum) (v.i. with abl.): to lean on.

innoxius, -a, -um: harmless.

innuō, -ere, -uī, -ūtum (v.i.): to give a nod to, sign to.

inquam (def. verb): I say; inquit: he, she, it says.

inquiētus, -a, -um: restless.

innutrītus, -a, -um: nourished, brought up.

inrumpō, -ere, -rūpī, ruptum (v.t.): to break in.

insatiābiliter (adv.): insatiably.

īnserō, -ere, -seruī, -sertum (v.t.): to insert, mix with.

īnserō, -ere, -sēvī, -situm (v.t.): to sow, plant in.

īnsiliō, -īre, -uī (v.i.): to leap into, spring at.

īnsistō, -ere, -stitī (v.i.): to stand on.

īnsonō, -āre, -āvī, -ātum (v.i.): to make a sound.

īnstāns, -ntis: pressing, urgent.

īnstituō, -ere, -uī, -ūtum (v.t.): to train, educate.

īnstō, -āre, -stitī (v.i.): to stand in or on, impend.

īnstrumentum, -ī (n.): instrument, appliance.

īnstruō, -ere, -xī, -ctum (v.t.): to inform, instruct, draw up.

īnsum, -esse, -fuī (v.i.): to be in, be contained.

integer, -gra, -grum: fresh, entire, unharmed.

intendō, -ere, -dī, -tum or sum (v.t.): to stretch towards, direct.

intentiō, -ōnis (f.): attention, application.

intentē (adv.): attentively, intently.

intentus, -a, -um: attentive, attent upon.

inter (prep. with acc.): between, among.

interaestuō, -āre (v.i.): to bubble up at intervals.

interdiu (adv.): during the day, by day.

interdum (adv.): sometimes, occasionally.

interest (v. impers.): it is of importance.

interficiō, -ere, -fēcī, -fectum (v.t.): to kill.

interiaceō, -ēre (*v.i.*): to lie between.

interim (*adv.*): meanwhile.

interior, -ius (*compar. adj.*): inside, inner.

intermittō, -ere, -mīsī, -missum (*v.t.*): to leave off.

interpellātiō, -ōnis (*f.*): interruption.

interpretor, -ārī, -ātus sum: to explain, expound.

interrogō, -āre, -āvī, -ātum (*v.t.*): to ask, question, interrogate.

intersum, -esse, -fuī (*v.i.*): to be present at, take part in.

interveniō, -īre, -vēnī, -ventum (*v.i.*): to come in between or during.

intueor, -ērī, -itus sum (*v.i.*): to look on.

inūsitātus, -a, -um: unusual.

invalēscō, -ere, -uī: to grow strong.

invalidus, -a, -um: weak, infirm.

inveniō, -īre, -vēnī, -ventum (*v.t.*): to come upon, find.

invicem (*adv.*): in turn.

invitō, -āre, -āvī, -ātum (*v.t.*): to invite, summon.

iocus, -ī (*m.*): jest, joke.

ipse, -a, -um: self, very.

is, ea, id: that, this, he, she, it; **is quī**: he who.

iste, -a, -ud: that (of yours), this.

ita (*adv.*): so, thus; **ita . . . ut**: in such a way that.

itaque (*conj.*): and so, accordingly.

iter, itineris (*n.*): journey, road, way; **ex itinere**: out of the way, away from the road.

iterum (*adv.*): a second time, again.

iubeō, -ēre, iussī, iussum (*v.t.*): to order.

iūcundus, -a, -um: agreeable, delightful.

iudicium, iī (*n.*): judgment, trial.

iūdicō, -āre, -āvī, -ātum (*v.t.*): to judge, decide.

iungō, -ere, iunxī, iunctum (*v.t.*): to join.

iūs, iūris (*n.*): right, justice.

iuvenis, -is (*c.*): youth.

iuvō, -āre, iūvī, iūtum (*v.t.*): to help, assist.

Kalendae, -ārum (*f. plur.*): Kalends, first day of the month.

labor, -ōris (*m.*): work, toil, hardship.

laetus, -a, -um: glad.

laevus, -a, -um: left.

laguncula, -ae (*f.*): small flask or bottle.

lancea, -ae (*f.*): light spear, lance.

languidus, -a, -um: listless, sluggish.

lapis, -idis (*m.*): stone.

lascīvia, -ae (*f.*): playfulness, wantonness.

lassō, -āre, -āvī, -ātum (*v.t.*): to tire, weary.

lātitūdō, -inis (*f.*): breadth, width.

latrōcinium, -iī (*n.*): robbery, fraud.

latus, -eris (*n.*): side, flank.

lātus, -a, -um: broad.

laudō, -āre, -āvī, -ātum (*v.t.*): to praise.

laus, laudis (*f.*): praise.

lautus, -a, -um: splendid, sumptuous.

lavō, -āre, āvi, or lāvī, -ātum, lautum or lōtum (v.t. and i.): to wash, bathe.

laxō, -āre, -āvī, -ātum (v.t. and i.): to relax, slacken.

lectiō, -ōnis (f.): reading.

lectitō, -āre, -āvī, -ātum (v.t.): to read often, or eagerly.

lectus, -ī (m.): bed.

lēgātus, -ī (m.): ambassador, deputy.

legō, -ere, lēgī, lectum (v.t.): to choose, read, read aloud.

lentus, -a, -um: slow.

levis, -e: light.

leviter (adv.): lightly.

libellus, -ī (m.): pamphlet, little book, letter, libellous information.

libenter (adv.): willingly, cheerfully.

līber, -era, -erum: free.

liber, -brī (m.): book.

līberī, -ōrum (m.): children.

līberō, -āre, -āvī, -ātum (v.t.): to set free.

lībertus, -ī (m.): freedman, manumitted slave.

lībet, -ēre, libuit and libitum est (v. impers.): it pleases.

licet, -ēre, licuit (v. impers.): it is lawful, permitted, one may; (introducing a concession): although.

līmen, -inis (n.): threshold, entrance; (a concession) although.

līnum, -ī (n.): sail, cloth.

linteum, -ī (n.): linen cloth.

līs, lītis (f.): strife, dispute, lawsuit.

littera, -ae (f.): letter of alphabet: in plural: letter, despatch.

lītus, -oris (n.): shore.

locus, -ī (m.): place, chance.

longinquus, -a, -um: long, extensive, distant.

longus, -a, -um: long; longum est: it would be tedious.

lūdificor, -ārī, -ātus sum (v.t.): to mock, delude.

lūdus, -ī (m.): game, play, pastime.

lūmen, -inis (n.): light.

lūridus, -a, -um: wan, pale, yellow.

lux, lūcis (f.): light.

luxuria, -ae (f.): luxury.

lymphātus, -a, -um: distracted, crazy.

lyristēs, -ae (m.): lute-player, lyrist.

maciēs, -ēī (f.): leanness, emaciation.

maculōsus, -a, -um: spotted.

maestus, -a, -um: sad.

magister, -trī (m.): schoolmaster.

magnopere, magis, maximē: greatly, exceedingly; eo magis quod: all the more because.

magistrātus, -ūs (m.): magistrate.

magnitūdō, -inis (f.): greatness, vastness, extent.

magnus, -a, -um, maior, maximus: great, large.

maledicō, -ere, -dīxī, -dictum (v.t.): to revile, slander.

malum, -ī (n.): evil, misfortune.

malus, -a, -um: bad, evil.

mandātum, -ī (n.): charge, order.

maneō, -ēre, mansī, mansum (v.i.): to remain.

mānēs, -ium (m. plur.): spirits, ghosts.

manifestus, -a, um: plain, clear, evident.

mānsuētūdō, -inis (f.): tameness.

manus, ūs (f.): hand, band.

mare, maris (n.): sea.

margō, -inis (m. and f.): edge, border, margin.

māter, mātris (f.): mother.

māteria, -ae (f.): subject-matter, material.

maximē adv.): exceedingly, very.

meātus, -ūs (m.): passage, course.

mediocriter (adv.): moderately.

meditor, -ārī, -ātus sum (v.t. and i.): to ponder over, meditate.

medium, -iī (n.): middle.

medius, -a, -um: middle.

melior, -ius (compar. adj.): better.

meminī, -isse (v. def.): to remember.

memoria, -ae (f.): memory.

mēns, mentis (f.): mind.

mēnsa, -ae (f.): board, table.

mentior, -īrī, mentītus sum (v.t. and i.): to tell lies.

merces, -ēdis (f.): hire, pay, wages, salaries.

mergō, -ere, mersī, mersum (v.t.): to dip, plunge, sink.

merīdiānus, -a, -um: pertaining to midday, noon.

metus, -ūs (m.): fear.

meus, -a, -um: my, mine.

mī: voc. sing. masc. of meus.

mīlitō, -āre, -āvī, -ātum (v.i.): to perform military service.

mīlle (indecl. adj. in sing.) mīlia, ium (n. plur.): thousand, thousands.

ministerium, -iī (n.): office, ministry.

ministra, -ae (f.): deaconess.

minor, -ārī, -ātus sum (v.t.): to threaten.

minuō, -ere, -uī, -ūtum (v.t. and i.): to make smaller, lessen, diminish.

minūtus, -a, -um: little, small minute.

mīrāculum, -ī (n.): miracle, wonder.

mīrandus, -a, -um: wonderful.

mīror, -ārī, -ātus sum (v.t. and i.): to wonder at, be astonished.

mīrus, -a, -um: wonderful, strange.

misceō, -ēre, miscuī, mistum or mixtum (v.t.): to mix, mingle.

miser, -era, -erum: wretched, miserable.

miserātiō, -ōnis (f.): pity, compassion.

miseria, -ae (f.): wretchedness, misfortune.

miseror, -ārī, -ātus sum (v.t.): to pity.

mittō, -ere, mīsī, missum (v.t.): to send; dismiss from the mind.

modicus, -a, -um: moderate-sized.

modus, -ī (n.): method, manner.

molestus, -a, -um: irksome, troublesome, annoying.

moneō, -ēre, -uī, -itum (v.t.): to warn, advise.

mōns, montis (m.): mountain.

mōnstrum, -ī (n.): portent, omen.

mora, -ae (f.): delay, staying.

morbus, -ī (m.): disease, illness.

morior, -ī, mortuus sum (v.i.): to die.

moror, -arī, -ātus sum (v.t. and i.): to delay, stay, remain.

mors, mortis (f.): death.

mortālis, -e: mortal.

mōs, mōris (m.): habit, custom; (plur.) character.

mōtus, -ūs (*m.*): movement, disturbance, earthquake.

moveō, -ēre, mōvī, mōtum (*v.t.*): to move.

mox (*adv.*): soon, next.

mulier, -eris (*f.*): woman.

multō (*adv.*): by much, much.

multum (*adv.*): much.

multus, -a, -um: much; **multī, -ae, -a:** many.

mundus, -ī (*m.*): world.

mūniceps, -cipis (*c.*): inhabitant, citizen.

mūnicipium, -iī (*n.*): country town, free town.

mūnus, -eris (*n.*): gift.

mūtātiō, -ōnis (*f.*): change, alteration.

mūtō, -āre, -āvī, -ātum (*v.t.* and *i.*): to change.

mūtuus, -a, -um: mutual.

nam (*conj.*): for.

nārrō, -āre, -āvī, -ātum (*v.t.*): to relate, narrate.

nascor, -ī, nātus sum (*v.i.*): to be born.

nātālis, -e: natal, pertaining to birth; (sc. **diēs**): birthday.

natō, -āre, -āvī, -ātum (*v.i.*): to swim.

nātūra, -ae (*f.*): nature.

nāvigābilis, -ē: navigable.

nāvigō, -āre, -āvī, -ātum (*v.t.*): to sail.

navis, -is (*f.*): ship.

nē (*conj.*): lest, so that . . . not; **nē quandō:** lest ever, **nē . . . quidem** (*adv.*): not even; **nē . . . an** (*adv.*): whether . . . or.

nebula, -ae (*f.*): vapour, smoke, fog.

nec: see **neque.**

necessārius, -a, -um: necessary.

necessitās, -ātis (*f.*): necessity.

necessitūdō, -inis (*f.*): connection, friendship, intimacy.

neglegō, -ere, -lēxī, -lectum (*v.t.*): to neglect, disregard, overlook.

negō, -āre, -āvī, -ātum (*v.t.*): to deny, say . . . not, refuse.

nēmō (*irreg.*): no one, nobody.

nemorōsus, -a, -um: woody.

nēquāquam (*adv.*): by no means, not at all.

neque or **nec** (*conj.*): and not, nor; **neque . . . neque** (**nec . . . nec**): neither . . . nor.

nesciō, -īre, nescīvī or **nesciī, nescītum** (*v.t.*): to be ignorant, not to know.

neu or **nēve,=et nē:** nor; **nēve . . . nēve** (**neu . . . neu**): neither . . . nor.

neuter, -tra, -trum: neither of two.

niger, -ra, -rum: black.

nihil (*indecl. n.*): nothing; **nihil est:** there is no reason.

nihilō (*adv.* of **nihilum**): none.

nihilōminus (also **nihilō minus**) (*adv.*): nevertheless, notwithstanding.

nimius, -a, -um: too much, beyond measure, excessive.

nisi (*conj.*): unless, if not, except.

nīsus, -ūs (*m.*): pressure, effort.

nix, nivis (*f.*): snow.

nō, nāre, nāvī (*v.i.*): to swim.

nōmen, -inis (*n.*): name.

nōminō, -āre, -āvī, -ātum (*v.t.*): to name, mention.

nōn (*adv.*): not.

Nōnae, -arum (*f. plural*): the Nones of the month (5th or 7th).

nōndum (*adv.*): not yet.

nōnne (*adv.*): surely (in questions expecting the answer 'yes').

nōnnūllus, -a, -um: some, several.

nōs: we.

noscitō, -āre, -āvī, -ātum (v.t.): to know, recognise.

noscō, -ere, nōvī, nōtum (v.t.): to find out, get to know, learn; (perf.): know.

noster, -ra, -rum: our.

nota, -ae (f.): mark, brand.

notābilis, -e: remarkable, noteworthy.

notārius, -iī (m.): writer, secretary.

novitās, -ātis (f.): novelty, strangeness.

novus, -a, -um: new; novissimus, -a, -um: last, latest; novissimē: last of all, finally.

nox, noctis (f.): night.

nūbes, -is (f.): cloud.

nūbilus, -a, -um: cloudy, overcast.

nūdus, -a, -um: bare.

nūllus, -a, -um: no, not any.

nūmen, -inis (n.): divine power, divinity.

numerō, -āre, -āvī, -ātum (v.t.): to count, number.

numerus, -ī (m.): number.

numquam (adv.): never.

nunc (adv.): now.

nuntiō, -āre, -āvī, -ātum (v.t.): to announce, report.

nuntius, -iī (m.): messenger, news.

nūper (adv.): recently.

nusquam (adv.): nowhere, in no place.

obdūcō, -ere, -xī, -ctum (v.t.): to cover over.

obfirmō, -āre, -āvī, -ātum (v.t.): to make firm, steadfast.

obiectus, -ūs (m.): a putting against, lying before.

oblīdo, -ere, -sī, -sum (v.t.): tc squeeze together.

obscūrus, -a, -um: little known.

obsequium, -iī (n.): compliance.

observō, -āre, -āvī, -ātum (v.t.): to pay attention to regard, observe.

obsideō, -ēre, -sēdī, -sessum (v.i. and t.): to besiege, beset.

obstinātiō, -ōnis (f.): stubbornness.

obstō, -āre, -stitī, -statum (v.i.): to stand before, stand in the way of.

obstringō, -ere, -nxī, -ctum (v.t.): to bind, lay under an obligation.

obstruō, -ere, -strūxī, -structum (v.t.): to obstruct.

obtineō, -ēre, -tinuī, -tentum (v.t.): to hold, gain, acquire.

obterō, -ere, -trīvī, -trītum (v.t.): to crush, trample on.

obversor, -ārī, -ātus sum (v.t.): to move about, go to and fro.

obvius, -a, -um: met, encountered.

occidēns, -ntis (m.): the west.

occidō, -ere, -cidī, -cāsum (v.i.): to fall, go down, perish, die.

occultē (adv.): secretly, privately.

occupātiō, -ōnis (f.): employment, occupation.

occurrō, -ere, -currī, -cursum (v.i.): to hasten, go to meet, run.

occursō, -āre, -āvī, -ātum (v.t.): to run, go or come to meet.

oculus, -ī (m.): eye.

odor, -ōris (m.): smell, odour.

offerō, -ferre, obtulī, oblātum (v.t.): to present, offer, meet, encounter.

ōminor, -ārī, -ātus sum (v.t.): to predict, prophesy.

omnīnō (*adv.*): altogether, wholly.

omnis, -e: all, every.

onerōsus, -a, -um: burdensome.

opācus, -a, -um: shady, cool.

opera, -ae (*f.*): pain, exertion, trouble, attention.

operiō, -īre, -uī, -ertum (*v.t.*): to cover.

opīnor, -ārī, -ātus sum (*v.i.*): to think, consider.

oppidum, -ī (*n.*): town.

opportūnē (*adv.*): fitly, seasonably.

opportūnus, -a, -um: fit, timely, opportune.

optimus, -a, um: best, very good.

optō, -āre, -āvī, -ātum (*v.t.*): to desire, wish for.

opus, -eris (*n.*): work; opus est: there is need of.

opusculum, -ī (*n.*): a little work.

ōrātiō, -ōnis (*f.*): speech, oration.

orbis, -is (*m.*): earth, globe; orbis terrārum: the world.

ordō, -inis (*m.*): order, rank, grade.

oriēns, -ntis (as *subt. m.*): the rising sun, east.

orior, -īrī, ortus sum (*v.i.*): to arise.

ornō, -āre, -āvī, -ātum (*v.t.*): to decorate, adorn, honour.

ōrō, -āre, -āvī, -ātum (*v.t.*): to beg, pray.

os, ossis (*n.*): a bone.

ostendō, -ere, -dī, -sum or -tum (*v.t.*): to show.

ōtiōsus, -a, -um: without employment, idle, useless.

ōtium, -iī (*n.*): freedom, 1est, leisure.

paedagōgium, -iī (*n.*): a pages' hall where children of lowly birth lived.

paenitentia, -ae (*f.*): repentance.

paenitet, -ēre, paenituit (*v. impers.*): to repent.

pānārium, -iī (*n.*): bread basket.

pannus, -ī (*m.*): piece of cloth.

par, paris (*adj.*): equal.

parātus, -a, -um: ready, prepared.

pariēs, -etis (*m.*): wall of a room.

parcō, -ere, pepercī, parsum (*v.i.* with *dat.*): to spare.

parēns, -ntis (*c.*): a parent.

pareō, -ēre, -uī, -itum (*v.i.* with *dat.*): to obey.

pariter (*adv.*): equally.

parō, -āre, -āvī, -ātum (*v.t.*): to prepare.

pars, partis (*f.*): part, direction.

parum (*adv.*): too little.

parvulus, -a, -um: very small.

parvus, -a, -um: small.

passim (*adv.*): everywhere.

pater, patris (*m.*): father.

patēscō, -ere, -uī (*v.i.*): to be laid open, open.

patientia, -ae (*f.*): patience, endurance.

patior, -ī, passus sum (*v.t.*): to endure, suffer, allow.

patria, -ae (*f.*): native land; (VIII 10) at home, in my home town.

pauculus, -a, um: very few, very little.

paucus, -a, -um: few, little (mostly in *plur.*).

paulātim (*adv.*): little by little, by degrees.

paulō (*adv.*): somewhat.

paulum (*adv.*): a little, somewhat.

pavor, -ōris (*m.*): fear, dread, alarm.

pecunia, -ae (*f.*): money.

per (*prep.* with *acc.*): through, along, by means of.

peragō, -ere, -ēgī, -āctum (*v.t.*): to perform, finish.

percunctor, -ārī, -ātus sum (*v.t.*): to enquire closely, investigate.

perdō, -ere, -didī, -ditum (*v.t.*): to destroy, ruin, lose.

peregrē (*adv.*): in a foreign place, abroad.

pereō, -īre, -iī, -itum (*v.i.*): to perish, be killed.

perferō, -ferre, -tulī, -lātum (*v.t.*): to bring, deliver, endure.

pergrātus, -a, -um: very agreeable, very pleasant.

periclitor, -ārī, -ātus sum (*v.i.*): to incur danger.

perīculum, -ī (*n.*): danger.

permaneō, -ēre, -mānsī, -mansum (*v.i.*): to remain, continue.

permūtō, -āre, -āvī, -ātum (*v.t.*): to change, alter.

perpetuus, -a, -um: perpetual, continuous.

perquam (*adv.*): extremely, completely.

perseverō, -āre, -āvī, -ātum (*v.i.* and *t.*): to persist, continue, persevere.

perspicuus, -a, -um: clear, transparent.

perstō, -āre, -stitī, -stātum (*v.i.*): to stand firmly.

perterritus, -a, -um: terrified.

pertinācia, -ae (*f.*): obstinacy, persistency.

pertrectō, -āre, -āvī, -ātum (*v.t.*): to touch, handle.

pervagor, -ārī, -ātus sum (*v.i.* and *t.*): to wander through, pervade.

pēs, pedis (*m.*): foot.

pessimus, -a, -um: very bad.

pestilēns, -ntis: pestilential, infected.

petō, -ere, petīvī, petītum (*v.t.*): to seek, ask, strike out for.

phantasma, -atis (*n.*): spectre, apparition.

philosophus, -ī (*m.*): philosopher.

pietās, -ātis (*f.*): dutiful conduct, affection, piety.

pīnus, -ūs or **ī** (*f.*): a pine tree.

piscor, -ārī, -ātus sum (*v.i.*): to fish.

placeō, -ēre, -cuī, -citum (*v.i.*): to please; **placet** (*impers. verb* and *dat.*): it pleases.

plānē (*adv.*): simply, plainly.

plānus, -a, -um: level, flat.

plēnus, -a, -um: full, filled with (with genit.).

plērīque, pleraeque, pleraque: most, very many.

plērumque (*adv.*): generally, for the most part.

plūs, plūris: more; **plūres**: the majority (*superl.* **plūrimus, -a, -um**).

poēticus, -a, -um: poetical.

polliceor, -ērī, -itus sum (*v.t.* and *i*): to promise, offer.

pondus, -eris (*n.*): weight.

pōnō, -ere, posuī, positum (*v.t.*): to place, put.

pōns, pontis (*m.*): bridge.

populus, -ī (*m.*): people, nation.

pōpulus, -ī (*f.*): poplar tree.

porticus, -ūs (*f.*): colonnade, portico.

poscō, -ere, poposcī (*v.t.*): to demand.

possum, posse, potuī (*v.i.*): to be able, to have power.

post (*prep.* with *acc.*): after, behind; (*adv.*): after.

posteā (*adv.*): afterwards.

posterus, -a, -um: next, following. **posterī:** those to come, descendants.

postquam (*conj.*): after.

postrēmō (*adv.*): finally, lastly.

potestās, -ātis (*f.*): power.

potissimum (*superl. adv.*): especially, principally, chiefly.

praebeō, -ēre, -uī, -itum (*v.t.*): to offer, afford.

praecēdō, -ere, -cessī, -cessum (*v.t.*): to go before, precede, excel.

praeceptor, -ōris (*m.*): teacher.

praeceptum, -ī (*n.*): rule, maxim, direction.

praecipiō, -ere, -cēpī, -ceptum (*v.t.*): to instruct, order.

praecipuē (*adv.*): especially, chiefly, particularly.

praeclārus, -a, -um: famous, distinguished, splendid.

praecursōrius, -a, -um: precursory.

praedicātiō, -ōnis (*f.*): praising, commendation.

praedium, -iī (*n.*): property, farm, estate.

praeeō, -īre, -īvī or **-iī, -itum** (*v.i.*): to precede in writing, dictate.

praeferō, -ferre, -tulī, -lātum (*v.t.*): to prefer, place before.

praemoneō, -ēre, -uī, -itum (*v.t.*): to advise, forewarn.

praenuntia, -ae (*f.*): foreteller, harbinger.

praenuntius, -iī (*m.*): foreteller, harbinger.

praesēns, -ntis: present, ever present.

praestō, -āre, -stitī, -statum or **-stitum** (*v.t.*): to show, display.

praetendō, -ere, -dī, -tum (*v.t.*): to extend; **praetendere auribus:** to concentrate.

praeter (*prep.* with *acc.*): besides, except.

praetereā (*adv.*): besides, moreover.

praeteritus, -a, -um: past.

praetexta, -ae (*f.*): the *toga praetexta*, or toga worn by boys and edged with purple.

praetextātus, -a, -um: wearing the *toga praetexta*.

praetūra, -ae (*f.*): the office of praetor.

praevaleō, -ēre, -uī (*v.i.*): to have greater power, to prevail.

prāvus, -a, -um: crooked, depraved, absurd.

precor, -ārī, -ātus sum (*v.i.* and *t.*): to pray, beseech, entreat.

premō, -ere, pressī, pressum (*v.t.*): to press.

pretium, -iī (*n.*): price, worth, value.

prīmō, prīmum (*adv.*): first, firstly.

prīmus, -a, -um: first; **in prīmīs:** especially, chiefly.

prior, -ōris (compar. adj.): former, first (of two).

priscus, -a -um: ancient.

prius (*adv.*): before, sooner: **priusquam** or **prius quam** (*conj.*): before.

prīvātus, -a -um: private

prō (*prep.* with *abl.*): on behalf of, instead of.

probō, -āre, -āvī, ātum (*v.t.*): to approve, prove.

prōcēdō, -ere, -cessī, -cessum (*v.i.*): to advance, go forward.

prōcōnsul, -cōnsulis (*m.*): a proconsul, military commander, provincial commander.

procul (*adv.*): afar off.

prŏcurrō, -ere, -currĭ or -cucurrĭ, -cursum (v.i.): to run forward.

prŏdūcō, -ere, -dūxĭ, -ductum (v.t.): to bring out, extend, project, lead forward.

profānus, -a, -um: not sacred.

prōficĭō, -ere, -fēcĭ, -fectum (v.i. and t.): to gain ground, make way.

proficiscor, -ī, -fectus sum (v.i.): to set out, start, travel.

proiciō, -ere, -iēcĭ, -iectum (v.t.): to throw away.

proinde (adv.): hence, thence, accordingly, just so.

promiscuus, -a, -um: common, ordinary.

promissus, -a, -um: long, hanging down.

prōnuntiō, -āre, -āvĭ, -ātum (v.t.): to proclaim, announce.

prope (prep. with acc.): near; (adv.): nearly; propius, proximē: nearer, nearest.

properō, -āre, -āvĭ, -ātum (v.t. and i.): to hasten, hurry.

prōpōnō, -ere, -posuĭ, -positum (v.t.): to expose, display, describe.

proprius, -a, -um: one's own, special, particular.

prōripiō, -ere, -ripuĭ, -reptum (v.t.): to rush out, hasten.

propter (prep. with acc.): on account of, because of.

prōscrībō, -ere, -scrīpsĭ, -scriptum (v.t.): to post up, advertise for sale.

prospectō, -āre, -āvĭ, -ātum (v.t.): to look at, view.

prōsum, prodesse: prōfuĭ (v.i.): to benefit, be of use to.

prout (adv.): just as, as.

prōvehō, -ere, -vexĭ, -vectum (v.t.): to carry forward.

prōvincia, -ae (f.): province.

proximē (adv.): nearest, next: last; proximus, -a, -um, nearest, next, last.

prudentia, -ae (f.): intelligence, prudence.

publicē (adv.): at the cost of the state.

pūblicō, -āre, -āvĭ, -ātum (v.t.): to publish.

pūblicus, -a, -um: public.

pudīcus, -a, -um: modest, chaste.

pudor, -ōris (m.): shame.

puer, -erī (m.): boy.

puerīliter (adv.): childishly.

pueritia, -ae (f.): childhood, boyhood.

pugillāres, -ium (m. plur.) sc. libelli: writing tablets.

pulcher, -ra, -rum: beautiful.

pūmex, -icis (m.): pumice, -stone.

pūniō, -īre, -īvĭ or -iĭ, -ītum (v.t.): to punish.

pūrus, -a, -um: pure.

putō, -āre, -āvĭ, -ātum (v.t.): to think, believe, suppose.

putrefaciō, -ere, -fēcĭ, -factum (v.t.): to make rotten, cause to putrefy.

quaerō, -ere, -sīvĭ, -sītum (v.t.): to seek, search for, ask.

quaestor, -ōris (m.): quaestor.

qualis, -e: of what nature, of such a kind.

qualiscunque, qualecunque: whosoever, whatsoever.

quam (adv.): how, than; quam with superlatives: as . . . as possible.

quamlibet (adv.): however.

quamquam (conj.): although; (V 26) even.

quamvīs (adv.): however much, although.

quandō (*adv.* and *conj.*): when?
si quando: if ever.
quandōque (*adv.*): at some time or other.
quantulus, -a, -um: how little, how small.
quantus, -a, -um: how much.
quartus, -a, -um: fourth.
quasi (*adv.*): as if.
quātenus (*adv.*): how far.
quatiō, -ere, no *perf.*, **quassum** (*v.t.*): to shake.
-que (*enclitic conj.*): and.
quemadmodum (also **quem ad modum**) (*adv.*): how.
querēla, -ae (*f.*): complaining, complaint.
quī (*adv.*): how.
quī, quae, quod: who, which; **est quod:** it is why; **quod prius:** as before.
quia (*conj.*): because.
quīcunque, quaecunque, quodcunque: whoever, whatever, whosoever, whatsoever.
quīdam, quaedam, quoddam: a certain; (*plur.*) some.
quidem (*adv.*): indeed.
quies, -ētis (*f.*): rest, quiet, repose.
quiescō, -ere, quiēvī, quiētum (*v.i.*): to rest, keep quiet.
quīlibet, quaelibet, quodlibet: anyone, anything.
quīntus, -a, -um: fifth.
quirītātus, -ūs (*m.*): wailing, shrieking.
quis, quid (*interr. pron.*): who? what? **quid** (*adv.*) why?
quis, quid (*indef. pron.*): anyone, anything, someone, something.
quisque, quaeque, quodque (*indef. pron.*): each, every.
quisquis, quaeque, quodquod: whosoever, whatsoever.
quō magis: all the more.

quō propius: the nearer.
quod (*conj.*): because.
quoque (*conj.*): also.
quorsum (*adv.*): to what purpose?
quotiēns (*adv.*): how often?, how many times?

rāmus, -ī (*m.*): branch, bough.
rārō (*adv.*): rarely.
rārus, -a, -um: rare, few, infrequent.
ratiō, -ōnis (*f.*): reason, reckoning, account.
recēdō, -ere, -cessī, -cessum (*v.i.*): to withdraw, retire, depart.
recēns, -ntis (*adj.*): fresh.
receptāculum, -ī (*n.*): refuge, retreat.
recīdō, -ere, -recīdī, recīsum (*v.t.*): to cut away, cut down.
recipiō, -ere, -cēpī, -ceptum (*v.t.*): to take back, recover, receive; **sē recipere:** to withdraw, retreat.
recitō, -āre, -āvī, -ātum (*v.t.*): to read out, recite.
recordor, -ārī, -ātus sum (*v.t.* and *i.*): to recall, remember.
rēctē (*adv.*): rightly.
rēctus, -a, -um: straight, upright.
recubō, -are (*v.i.*): to recline.
recumbō, -ere, -cubuī (*v.i.*): to lie down, recline at table.
recūsō, -āre, -āvī, -ātum (*v.t.*): to refuse, decline, object to.
reddō, -ere, reddidī, redditum (*v.t.*): to return, restore.
redigō, -ere, redēgī, redāctum (*v.t.*): to bring back, reduce, lessen.
redormiō, -īre (*v.i.*): to sleep again.

redūcō, -ere, -dūxī, -ductum (v.t.): to lead back.

referō, -ferre, rettulī, relātum (v.t.): to bring back, report, notify.

rēfert (impers.): it matters.

reficiō, -ere, -fēcī, -fectum (v.t.): to refresh, restore, repair.

refugiō, -ere, fūgi (v.t. and i.): to flee back, run away.

regō, -ere, rēxī, rēctum (v.t.): to rule.

regredior, -ī, regressus sum (v.i.): to return, retreat.

rēligiō, -ōnis (f.): religious scruple or obligation.

rēligiōsus, -a, -um: pious, devout.

relinquō, -ere, -līquī, -lictum (v.t.): to leave, abandon.

reliquus, -a, -um: remaining, left.

relūceō, -ēre -xī (v.i.): to shine back, shine out, grow light.

remaneō, -ēre, -mansī (v.i.): to stay or remain behind.

remedium, -iī (n.): remedy, cure.

remittō, -ere, -mīsī, -missum (v.t.): to send back, yield, resign.

rēmus, -ī (m.): oar.

repellō, -ere, reppulī, repulsum (v.t.): to drive back.

repentē (adv.): suddenly.

repentīnus, -a, -um: sudden, unexpected.

reperiō, -īre, repperī, repertum (v.t.): to find, perceive.

repetō, -ere, -petīvī, -petītum (v.t.): to ask back, seek again.

reportō, -āre, -āvī, -ātum (v.t.): to bring back.

repraesentō, -āre, -āvī, -ātum (v.t.): to show, exhibit.

reprehendō, -ere, -dī, -sum (v.t.): to reprove, find fault with.

reprimō, -ere, -pressī, -pressum (v.t.): to repress, keep back.

requiēs, -ētis (f.): rest, repose.

requīrō, -ere, -quīsīvī, -quīsītum (v.t.): to seek out, request, look in vain for.

rēs, rēī (f.): thing, affair, matter, event, circumstance.

rēspublica, -ae (f.): public, official business, state, politics.

resideō, -ēre, -sēdī (v.i.): to sit down, remain sitting.

resorbeō, -ēre (v.t.): to suck, back, swallow again.

respiciō, -ere, -spexī, -spectum (v.t. and i.): to look back at.

respondeō, -ēre, -dī, -sum (v.i.): to answer, reply.

resumō, -ere, -sūmpsī, -sumptum (v.t.): to take up again, resume.

rētē, -is (n.): net.

retineō, -ēre, -tinuī, -tentum (v.t.): to keep back, retain.

retractō, -āre, -āvī, -ātum (v.t.): to take hold of, handle again.

retractātus, -a, -um: lying back, remote, distant.

retrō (adv.): backwards.

reus, -ī (m.): defendant, accused.

rēvērā (adv.): in truth.

revertor, -ī, -versus sum (v.i.): to turn back, return.

revocō, -āre, -āvī, -ātum (v.t.): to recall, restore.

revolvō, -ere, -volvī, -volūtum (v.t.): to roll back, unroll.

rīdeō, -ēre, rīsī, rīsum (v.i. and t.): to laugh, laugh at.

rigor, -ōris (m.): stiffness, coldness, numbness.

rīpa, -ae (f.): bank of a stream.

rīte (adv.): with due observance, fitly, rightly.

rōbustus, -a, -um: strong, fit, hardy.

rogō, -āɪ.., -āvī, -ātum (v.t.): to ask, implore.

ruīna, -ae (f.): fall, landslide.

rumpō, -ere, rūpī, ruptum (v.t.): to break, burst, tear.

ruō, -ere, ruī, rutum (v.i.): to fall, rush down, go to ruin.

rūrsus (adv.): again, back again, in turn.

S:=abbreviation for **Salūtem dat**=gives greeting to.

sacellum, -ī (n.): chapel.

sacer, -ra, -rum: sacred.

sacramentum, -ī (n.): oath, solemn obligation.

saeculum, -ī (n.): age, generation, spirit of age.

saepe (adv.): often

salūs, -ūtis (f.): safety.

salūtō, -āre, -āvī, -ātum (v.t.): to pay one's respects.

salvus, -a, -um: safe, in good health.

sanctus, -a, -um: sacred, holy.

satis (adv.): enough; (comp): **satius:** better, rather; **satius est:** it would be better.

scelus, -eris (n.): crime, wickedness.

scientia, -ae (f.): knowledge.

scīlicet (adv.): of course, clearly.

sciō, scīre, scīvī, scītum (v.t.): to know.

scrībō, -ere, scrīpsī, scrīptum (v.t.): to write.

scrīnium, -ii (n.): a box for keeping letters, writing desk.

sē (sēsē): himself, herself, itself, themselves.

sēcum: with himself, etc.

sēcēdō, -ere, -cessī, -cessum (v.i.): to go to, withdraw, retire.

sēcrētum, -ī (n.): solitude, retreat.

secundum (prep. with acc.): along, by, according to.

secundus, -a, -um: favourable, successful.

sēcūritās, -ātis (f.): freedom from care, unconcern, composure.

sēcūrus, -a, -um: free from care, composed.

sed (conj.): but.

sedeō, -ēre, sēdī, sessum (v.i.): to sit.

segnis, -e: slow, idle, inactive.

semel (adv.): once.

semper (adv.): always.

senēscō, -ere, senuī (v.i.): to grow old.

senex, senis (m.): old man.

sēparō, -āre, -āvī, -ātum (v.t.): to divide, separate.

sepeliō, -īre, -īvī, sepultum (v.t.): to bury.

September, -bris, -bre: September.

septimus, -a, -um: seventh.

sequor, -ī, secūtus sum (v.t.): to follow.

serēnus, -a, -um: bright, clear, fair; **serēnum, -i** (n.): bright weather.

sermō, -ōnis (m.): talk, conversation.

serpō, -ere, -psī, -ptum (v.i.): to creep, crawl.

servō, -āre, -āvī, -ātum (v.t.): to keep safe, preserve.

servulus, -ī (m.): a young slave.

seu or **sīve** (conj.): whether . . . or.

sevēritās, -ātis (f.): seriousness, sternness.

sexus, -ūs (m.): sex.

sī (conj.): **sī quandō:** if ever; **sī quis:** if anyone.

siccō, -āre, -āvī, -ātum (*v.t.*): to dry.

siccus, -a, -um: dry.

significō, -āre, -āvī, -ātum (*v.t.*): to make a mark or sign.

signum, -ī (*n.*): sign.

silentium, -ī (*n.*): silence.

sileō, -ēre, -uī (*v.i.* and *t.*): to be silent, keep silence.

silva, -ae (*f.*): wood, forest.

similis, -e: like.

similitūdō, -inis (*f.*): likeness, resemblance.

simul (*adv.*): at the same time.

simulācrum, -ī (*n.*): likeness, image.

sine (*prep.* with *abl.*): without.

siphō, -ōnis (*m.*): fire engine.

sistō, -ere, stitī, statum (*v.t.* and *i.*): to stop, arrest.

societās, -ātis (*f.*): fellowship, association, partnership.

sōl, sōlis (*m.*): sun.

solācium, -iī (*n.*): consolation.

solea, -ae (*f.*): sandal.

soleō, -ēre, solitus sum (*v.i.*): to be accustomed.

solemne, -is (*n.*): usage, custom, practice.

sōlitūdō, -inis (*f.*): loneliness, solitude.

sollicitō, -āre, -āvī, -ātum (*v.t.*): to incite, stir up, win over.

sollicitūdō, -inis (*f.*): anxiety.

sōlor, -ārī, -ātus sum (*v.t.*): to console.

solum, -ī (*n.*): earth, soil.

sōlum (*adv.*): only, alone; **nōn sōlum . . . sed etiam** (**nōn sōlum . . . verum etiam**): not only . . . but also.

sōlus, -a, -um: alone, only.

solūtus, -a, -um: free from.

solvō, -ere, solvī, solūtum (*v.t.*): to loosen.

solvere (navem solvere): to set sail, sail out.

somnus, -ī (*m.*): sleep.

sonō, -āre, sonuī, sonitum (*v.i.* and *t.*): to make a noise, sound.

sonus, -ī (*m.*): sound.

sordēs, -is (*f.*): dirt, filth, meanness.

sordidus, -a, um: mean.

sors, sortis (*f.*): lot.

spargō, -ere, sparsī, sparsum (*v.t.*): to scatter, sprinkle.

spatior, -ārī, spatiātus sum (*v.i.*): to walk.

spatiōsus, -a, -um: spacious.

spatium, -iī (*n.*): space.

speciēs, -ēī (*f.*): appearance, semblance.

spectāculum, -ī (*n.*): sight, show.

spectō, -āre, -āvī, -ātum (*v.t.*): to look at.

spectator, -ōris (*m.*): spectator.

speculāria, -ōrum (*n. pl.*): window panes, a window.

spērō, -āre, -āvī, -ātum (*v.t.*): to hope for, hope, expect.

spēs, spēī (*f.*): hope.

spīritus, -ūs (*m*): vapour, breath of air.

squālor, -ōris (*m*): dirt squalor.

stagnum, -ī (*n*): pond, pool.

statim (*adv.*): immediately, at once.

statuō, -ere, -uī, -ūtum (*v.t.*): to decide, conclude, determine, arrange.

status, -a, -um: fixed, appointed, settled.

sternō, -ere, strāvī, strātum (*v.t.*): to spread out, strew, lay low.

stilus, -ī (*m.*): pen.

(stips) stipis (*f.*): gift, donation, small coin.

stō, stāre, stetī, statum (*v.i.*): to stand.

stomachus, -ī (*m.*): stomach, windpipe, digestion, displeasure.

strepitus, -ūs (*m.*): noise, din.

studeō, -ēre, -uī (*v.i.*): to be eager for, wish, desire, study.

studium, iī (*n.*): eagerness, zeal, attachment.

suādeō, -ēre, suāsī, suāsum (*v.i. and t.*): to persuade.

suāvitās, -ātis (*f.*): sweetness.

sub (*prep.* with *acc.* or *abl.*): under, beneath, below.

subeō, -īre, -iī, -itum (*v.i. and t.*): to come up, spring up.

subiaceō, -ēre, -uī, (*v.i.*): to lie under, lie near.

subitus, -a, -um: sudden, unexpected.

submittō, -ere, -mīsī, -missum (*v.t.*): to cut off.

subsistō, -ere, -stitī (*v.t. and i.*): to stop, stay.

subter (*prep.* with *acc.*): beneath, at the foot of.

subveniō, -īre, -vēnī, -ventum (*v.i.*): to come to aid, help.

sufficiō, -ere, -fēcī, -fectum (*v.t. and i.*): to afford, furnish, suffice.

sulfur, -uris (*n.*): sulphur.

sum, esse, fuī: to be.

summa, -ae (*f.*): sum, total.

summus, -a, -um: highest, greatest, very great.

sūmō, -ere, sūmpsī, sūmptum (*v.t.*): to take, take up.

sūmptuōsus, -a, -um: expensive, costly.

sūmptus, -ūs (*m.*): expense, cost.

super (*prep.* with *acc.*): above.

superfundō, -ere, -fūdī, -fūsum (*v.t.*): to pour, pour over.

superō, -āre, -āvī, -ātum (*v.t.*): to overcome, conquer.

superstes, -stitis: surviving.

superstitiō, -ōnis (*f.*): superstition.

supersum, -esse, -fuī (*v.i.*): to remain over, survive.

supplicium, -iī (*n.*): punishment.

supplicō, -āre, -āvī, ātum (*v.i.*): to beseech, supplicate.

supprimō, -ere, -pressī, -pressum (*v.t.*): to keep back, detain, suppress.

surgō, -ere, surrexī, surrectum (*v.i. and t.*): to arise.

suspēnsus, -a, -um: suspended, raised, elevated.

suspiciō, -ere, -spexī, -spectum (*v.t. and i.*): to mistrust, suspect.

suus, -a, -um: his, her, its, their own.

tālis, -e, such, of such a kind.

tālis . . . quālis: such . . . as.

tam (*adv.*): so, so much; **tam . . . quam:** so . . . as, as . . . as.

tamen (*adv.*): nevertheless, however, yet.

tametsī (*conj.*): although.

tamquam (*adv.*): as if, just as.

tangō, -ere, tetigī, tāctum (*v.t.*): to touch, border on.

tantum (*adv.*): so much, only.

tantus, -a, -um: so great, so large.

tarditās, -ātis (*f.*): slowness, tardiness.

tardus, -a, -um: late.

tectum, -ī (*n.*): roof, house.

temperō, -āre, -āvī, -ātum (*v.t. and i.*): to restrain, check, regulate.

tempestās, -ātis (*f.*): storm, weather.

templum, -ī (*n.*): temple.

tempus, -oris (*n.*): time.

tendō, -ere, tetendī, tēnsum or **tentum** (*v.t.* and *i.*): to stretch, make for.

tenebrae, -ārum (*f. plur.*): darkness, night.

teneō, -ēre, -uī, tentum (*v.t.*): to hold, keep.

tener, -era, -erum: young, inexperienced, tender.

tenuis, -e: thin, fine, in low circumstances.

tenuō -āre, -āvī, -ātum (*v.t.*): to make thin, dilute.

tergum, -ī (*n.*): back, rear.

terminus, -ī (*m.*): boundary, limit.

terra, -ae (*f.*): land, earth.

terribilis, -e: frightful, terrible.

terrificus, -a, um: causing terror, frightful.

terror, -ōris (*m.*): dread, fright, alarm.

tertiō (*adv.*): for a third time.

tertius, -a, -um: third.

timeō, -ēre, -uī (*v.t.* and *i.*): to fear, be alarmed.

timor, -ōris (*m.*): fear, panic.

titulus, -ī (*m.*): placard, notice.

tollō, -ere, sustulī, sublātum (*v.t.*): to raise, take up, abolish.

tondeō, -ēre, totondī, tōnsum (*v.t.*): to shear, cut, clip.

tormentum, -ī (*n.*): anguish, pain.

torqueō, -ēre, torsī, tortum (*v.t.*): to twist, turn.

torrēns, -ntis: hot, burning, rushing.

torreō, -ēre, torruī, tostum (*v.t.*): to parch, roast, bake, burn.

tortus, -a, -um: twisted.

torus, -ī (*m.*): couch, bed.

tot (*indecl. adj.*): so many.

totidem (*adv.*): as many times.

tōtus, -a, -um: whole, entire.

tractātus, -ūs (*m.*): touching, handling.

tractō, -āre, -āvī, -ātum (*v.t.*): to manage, treat, handle.

trahō, -ere, trāxī, tractum (*v.t.*): to drag, draw.

trānseō, -īre, -iī, -itum (*v.i.* and *t.*): to go over, cross.

trānsferō, -ferre, -tulī, -lātum (*v.t.*): to carry across, transfer.

trānsmittō, -ere, -mīsī, -missum (*v.t.* and *i.*): to send or convey across, transmit.

tremor, -ōris (*m.*): shaking, tremor, earthquake.

trepidātiō, -ōnis (*f.*): alarm, agitation.

trepidō, -āre, -āvī, -ātum (*v.t.* and *i.*): to hurry anxiously, be in a state of alarm.

trēs, tria: three.

tribūnātus, -ūs (*m.*): tribuneship.

trīclīnium, -iī (*n.*): dining-room, triclinium.

triennium, -iī (*n.*): period of three years.

trīstis, -e: sad, melancholy, stern.

truncus, -ī (*m.*): trunk of a tree.

tū: you.

tum (*adv.*): at that time, then.

tunc (*adv.*): at that very time, then.

tunica, -ae (*f.*): tunic.

turba, -ae (*f.*): crowd, uproar.

turpis, -ē: disgraceful, base.

tūs, tūris (*n.*): incense.

tūtēla, -ae (*f.*): watching, protection, wardship, guardianship.

tuus, -a, -um: your.

ubi (*adv.* or *conj.*): when, where?

ubīque (*adv.*): everywhere.

ūllus, -a, -um: any.

ūltrā (*adv.* or *prep.* with *acc.*): further, more, beyond: (*compar.*) ulterior.

ululātus, -ūs (*m.*): wailing, shrieking.

ūnā (*adv.*): together.

unde (*adv.*): where from, whence.

undique (*adv.*): from all sides, on every side.

ungō (unguō), -ere, unxī, (*v.t.*): to anoint, smear.

unguentum, -ī (*n.*): ointment, perfume.

ūniversus, -a, -um: all together, entire, whole.

in ūniversum: in general, generally.

ūnus, -a, -um: one, only, alone.

urbānus, -a, -um: refined, elegant, belonging to the city.

urbs, urbis (*f.*): city (sometimes referring to the city of Rome).

ūsquam (*adv.*): anywhere.

ūsus, -ūs (*m.*): use, convenience, need, occasion.

ut (utī) (*adv.* and *conj.*): as, when, in order that, so that, (interrog) how?

utcumque (*adv.*): however, howsoever.

uterque, utraque: utrumque: both, each of two.

utinam (*adv.*): oh that! I wish that!

ūtor, ūtī, ūsus sum (*v.i.* with *abl.*): to use, practise, enjoy friendship of, enjoy.

utrum ... an: whether ... or.

uxor, -ōris (*f.*): wife.

vacuus, -a, -um: empty.

vadum, -ī (*n.*): shallow water, ford.

valē: farewell.

valeō, -ēre, -uī (*v.i.*): to be well, prevail.

validus, -a, -um: strong, healthy, well.

valvae, -ārum (*f. pl.*): folding door.

vānus, -a, -um: empty, void, vacant.

variō, -āre, -āvī, -ātum (*v.t.* and *i.*): to vary.

varius, -a, -um: varius, diverse.

vāstus, -a, -um: vast, enormous.

vāticinātiō, -ōnis (*f.*): foretelling, prediction.

vehementer (*adv.*): eagerly, vehemently.

vehiculum, -ī (*n.*): carriage, conveyance, vehicle.

vel (*conj.*): or; **vel ... vel:** either ... or.

vēlōcitās, -ātis (*f.*): speed.

vēlox, -ōcis: swift.

vēlum, -ī (*n.*): covering, curtain, sail.

velut (*adv.*): even as, just as, like.

vēna, -ae (*f.*): blood vessel, vein.

vēnābulum, -ī (*n.*): hunting spear.

vēnātiō, -ātiōnis (*f.*): hunting, chase.

vēneō, -īre, -īvī or iī, -itum (*v.i.*): to go for sale, to be sold.

venerātiō, -ōnis (*f.*): reverence, respect.

veneror, -ārī, -ātus sum (*v.t.*): to revere, reverence.

venia, -ae (*f.*): pardon.

veniō, -īre, vēnī, ventum (*v.i.*) to come.

venor, -ārī, -ātus sum (*v.t.* and *i.*): to hunt, chase.

ventus, -ī (*m.*): wind.

vēr, vēris (*n.*): the season of spring.

verbum, -ī (n.): word.
verēcundia, -ae (f.): shyness, bashfulness, modesty.
vereor, -ērī, veritus sum (v.t.): to respect, fear.
vērō (adv.): indeed, however, but.
versus, -ūs (m.): verse.
vērus, -a, -um: true; **vērum, -ī** (n.): the truth; **nec tantum . . . verum etiam**: not only . . . but also.
vertex, -icis (m.): top, crown of head.
vertō, -ere, vertī, versum (v.t.): to turn.
vespera, -ae (f.): evening.
vēstīgium, -iī (n.): track, trace, mark.
vestiō, -īre, -īvī, -ītum (v.t.): to clothe.
vetō, -āre, -uī, -itum (v.t.): to forbid.
vexō, -āre, -āvī, -ātum (v.t.): to harass, damage, harm.
via, -ae (f.): way, road, street.
viāticum, -ī (n.): travelling money.
vibrō, -ēre, -āvī, -ātum (v.t. and i.): to shake, agitate.
vice: instead of.
victima, -ae (f.): beast for sacrifice.
victor, -ōris (m.): victor, winner.
vīcus, -ī (m.): village, hamlet.
videō, -ēre, vīdī, vīsum (v.t.): to see; (pass.) to be seen, seem, appear.
vigil, -ilis: awake.
vigilia, -ae (f.): vigilance.
vigilō, -āre, -āvī, -ātum (v.t. and i.): to keep awake, watch.
vīgintī: twenty.
vīlis, -e: cheap.

vīlitās, -ātis (f.): cheapness.
vīlla, -ae (f.): country house, estate.
vincō, -ere, vīcī, victum (v.t.): to conquer.
vinculum, -ī (n.): chain.
vindicta, -ae (f.): the rod with which a slave was touched in the ceremony known as 'manumission', liberating-rod, punishment.
vīnum, -ī (n.): wine.
violentia, -ae (f.): violence.
vir, virī (m.): man.
viridis, -e: green; (viridia -ium (n. pl.): green plants, verdure.
virtūs, -ūtis (f.): courage, valour, merit, noble character.
vīs, vim, vī, pl. **vīrēs**: force power, (in pl.) strength.
vīsō, -ere, vīsī, vīsum (v.t.): to go to see, visit.
vīta, -ae (f.): life.
vitium, -iī (n.): fault, vice, crime.
vītō, -āre, āvī, -ātum (v.t.): to avoid.
vitreus, -a, -um: of glass, glassy.
vīvō, -ere, vīxī, victum (v.i.): to live.
vix (adv.): scarcely, hardly.
vocō, -āre, -āvi, -ātum (v.t.): to call, summon.
volō, velle, voluī (v.t. and i.): to wish, be willing.
volūptās, -ātis (f.): pleasure, delight.
vōs: you (plur.).
vōx, vōcis (f.): voice.
vulgus, -ī (n.): the common people, crowd.

xystus, -ī (m.): open colonnade or portico.